THE BOOK OF WAYS

The Book of Ways

COLIN WILL

RED SQUIRREL PRESS

First published in the UK in 2014 by
Red Squirrel Press
www.redsquirrelpress.com

Red Squirrel Press is distributed by Central Books Ltd.
and represented by Inpress Books Ltd.
www.inpressboks.co.uk

Designed and typeset by Gerry Cambridge
gerry.cambridge@btinternet.com
Cover images, 'Snipe's nest, Ayrshire,'
'Open Book', and 'Reeds reflecting in the
River Garnock', © Gerry Cambridge 2014

A CIP catalogue record is available from the British Library.

ISBN: 978 1 906700 97 3

Printed by Martins the Printers
www.martins-the-printers.co.uk

Acknowledgements

Versions of some of these poems have appeared in *Haibun Today* (www.haibuntoday.com), *Contemporary Haibun Online* (www. contemporaryhaibunonline.com), *The Road North* (http://the-road-north.blogspot.com) and *Notes from the Gean* (www. geantreepress.co.uk). The vast majority were written during the course of a Hawthornden Fellowship in 2013. I am deeply grateful to Hawthornden, its staff and its Admissions Committee for the time, space and environment this gave me to complete this book, for their wonderful hospitality, and for the excellent company of my fellow writers. I thank Brian Johnstone, Robyn Marsack, Alec Finlay, Andrew Forster, Lyn Moir, Ross Wilson and many other friends for their encouragement. I thank Alan Spence—our conversation about haibun led me to decide on a title. My special thanks to Gerry Loose for reading the manuscript so carefully. My publisher and friend Sheila Wakefield has given me unstinting encouragement throughout the project—every author should be lucky enough to find a publisher like her. Some of the European trips were biennial excursions, brilliantly organised by Bruce Jamieson, in the company of a large group of like-minded friends. Finally, I could not have written this book without the support of my wife Jane. She is the 'you' in many of these poems, and the other half of 'we' and 'us' for fifty years.

Contents

Section II

Section IV

What is haibun?

Japanese literature began with the tanka poem form in the 8th century, the first novels (by Sei Shonagon and Murasaki Shikibu) in the 10-11th centuries, and the linked-verse form renga in the 11th century, from which *hokku* and *haiku* later emerged. *Haibun* evolved from haiku.

The best known example of the form is Matsuo Basho's *Oku no Hosomichi*—Narrow Road to the Interior—a poetic record of a journey made in 1689. His friend and fellow poet Sora accompanied him on part of his journey, and they composed together in the manner of renga, with Basho's narrative interspersed with haiku. Many other Japanese writers have used the form since then, but its popularity in the West dates from the late 20th and early 21st century, when European and American writers discovered it for themselves.

So what exactly is it? The magazine *Haibun Today* has on its website a collection of diverse and often contradictory definitions. Basho simply says it is *haikai no bunsho*—writing in the style of haiku. Shiki's followers equate it with *shaseibun*—sketching in words. Most commentators agree on two things: they should contain prose written in the spirit of haiku; and they should contain, often as a conclusion, a haiku. The haiku should parallel but not epitomise the prose. 'The prose becomes the narrative of an epiphany, while the haiku is the epiphany itself.' (Bruce Ross: Narratives of the Heart, *World Haiku Review*, vol 1, 2002.)

Most haibun contain one haiku, some more, fewer none. The prose section is often, but not always, the record of a journey, real or allegorical. That has led some to characterise the haibun as a waybook, and that is the reason for the book's title. The risk is that a haibun collection becomes a series of travel notes, which I have tried hard to avoid: this is poetry.

You may think, given the flexibility of the form, that anything goes. Far from it. As with any other poetic form, there are techniques

—things which work and things which do not. There are skills to learn, and styles to develop. There are fashions too, especially in Western haibun. There's a recent tendency in some quarters to drastically shorten the prose sections, but I can see no logical reason for this, and it loses a lot of the poetry. The length of a haibun should depend solely on the needs of the narrative.

Some of these haibun relate to wanderings in other countries, but I've also included poems written at home in Scotland, together with poems reflecting my scientific background.

In this collection some haibun contain tanka and other short verse forms rather than haiku, but by and large the structure of prose plus one or more haiku has been adhered to, as has the 5-7-5 haiku structure. Some haiku are non-seasonal; some are closer to *senryu*, and many do not have the *kireji*—the cutting word. But there is precedent; Basho himself sometimes experimented in these ways. 'In the spirit of haiku' usually means present tense, direct speech, and first person narrative. I have mostly followed this, but occasionally I've used past tense. Sometimes I've used second person, making them conversations with my wife Jane, my companion along many of these ways. I think the form is robust enough to accommodate such diversions.

The collection has been cast in four parts, but the boundaries between them are flexible. The first poem is a non-linear reflection on places I've been, things I've seen or thought about, and forms an introduction to the first section. The second section features Scotland, wilderness (including mountains), and some travels; the third adds more travels plus some science-influenced poems; the fourth contains the most personal poems.

Colin Will
Hawthornden Castle and Dunbar
November 2013–February 2014

Section I

On reaching the Biblical span

Eliot's to thank
re-reading Gerontion
made me lift my pen

One

Here I am now, an old man, am qualified to say that. I'm mired
in memories, and my joints ache. I'd rather look forward than
back, but the sinuous past slithers to the top layer of the cortex.

The fence is mended that kept outsiders from looking in, but
now it has gaps, lines of sight where we can see the passers-by,
and therefore they can see us. We'll screen it with bushes, potted
shrubs, but nothing clinging, nothing to rot the nice new timber.

It was in that dire March before Desert Storm, with warplanes on
low-level training flights cutting Dunbar air into noisy slices, that I
painted the old fence red. I left the Labour Party then. And not looked
back. Lies—of course I have. Nearly forty years a member. Bound to.

> fixing the old fence
> the same as mending wall?
> keeping our lives screened
> keeping our thoughts to ourselves
> our histories separate

The snowdrops are dirty now, a single aconite—yellow cup, green
frills—sits on the mound of earth. Crocuses scatter colour over
the grey soil, daffodils without a Wordsworth in sight have not yet
broken open, momentarily they're yellow-tipped stalks, flanked
by starflowers. I know their botanical names, Latin epithets, but
why would I use them? Who else would know them? Colours are
limited, simplified, in this season, the way Hiroshige rendered
views around Edo, picturing the stations of the Tokaido.

Two

Where to next?

Madrid was Gallery City plus tapas. Velázquez, Goya, and Bosch
in the Prado, from the King's court to the Black Paintings, and the
Garden of Earthly Delights, so often seen in books, but here artist-
sized. I've stood in front of *Guernica*, stunned, in the Reina Sofia
gallery, and seen some marvellous works in the Thyssen Gallery.

Currywurst mit Pommes in Frankfurt Zoo, the zebra-striped small
plane, a memorial to Michael Grzimek, in the zebra enclosure, the
kingfisher on the branch over the water inside the tiger's soggy
paddock, the sun bears licking old tyres smeared with honey.

Oysters, stuffed quail, *iles flottante* in Brasserie Bofinger,
near l'Opera Bastille, our little hotel somewhere close in
the 12th *arrondissement*. At night I tried to read a street
map and first found my eyesight was failing. It wasn't until
a few years later that my hearing started to deteriorate.

> this is how we go
> senses failing one by one
> until we're senseless

The Abbaye at Fontevraud, the empty tombs of Henry
II, Eleanor of Aquitaine, Richard I, Lionheart, who died
nearby at Chinon, where we saw the *Fête Medieval*, the
roasting pig, the smoke, history as fancy dress, then back
on our bikes we continued our *circuit de degustation*.

We stay alive longer, so we need some latitude in the bands called
ages. When's middle age? What number do you put against 'old'?
Gerontion, where would you fit now? Between an earlier puberty
and the actuarial approach of maggots, we spread ourselves
thinner through time. Our money's thinner too. Of course I blame
the banks, the bankers, but greed's pretty universal, no? And
the red-tops are more effective than Pol Pot, or Mao's Cultural

Revolution, at reinforcing prejudice, dumbing down, suppressing attainment, ambition, glorying the cult of personality.

Three

In the beginning was the Planck Era, void without form, where there are no names for the infinitesimal parts of seconds. Then, give or take a yocto, quarks and anti-quarks whizzed about in a soup of bosons. Still no matter, until, after atoms formed, there was light—photons had room to move without infinities of collisions.

Asleep, then waking, time sometimes appears to run backwards. This morning I thought I had woken at 6:30, slept again until the clock showed 4:20, then lay awake through the fives and sixes —again, it seemed—until seven, when I could respectably rise.

So what happens next? I could sit here, on the Orion Arm of the Milky Way, near the Aquila Rift, looking for exo-planets, playing Beethoven's Ninth, as the world's crust spreads like finger nails, contemplating scenarios, mass extinctions, and my own. Better to move about, experience events, see what's out there, not what's in here, indexed in the amygdala for recall and relevance.

With Buddha it's the mind, not the man, that matters, so the focus is on thought, not treacherous histories.

> on the Eightfold Path
> follow your own line as far
> as it takes you

Belief's an odd bugger. Some things I take on trust, can't prove. Is that what belief is? If the smallest thing is true, and ten small things make one large, then that's true, and the world is true, and the way the world works is the way the world works. Complexity is only life not yet examined in sufficient detail. There is only the real, a fractal simplicity and a scale factor to set level of difficulty.

everything there is
to be touched, tasted, thought, proved
nothing else for me

Four

From the Basque refugia, after the Ice Age, coast-hoppers
travelled west and north, subsisting on shellfish and forage
from the fringing forest. Sooner or later settlements rooted in
favoured places, round-houses mushroomed along the western
shores. My ancestral folk lived and loved in Buchan, spoke a
Brythonic tongue. I've got that gene marker, the plain vanilla
ancient lineage without overprints; the bus pass to all the lost
dead nations and the lands before nations had names.

On windy nights, the window ventilators moan and howl
in a way I've come to find appropriate. What else can you
do against the wind, but summon noisy spirits?

Which malt tonight? Phenolic Laphroaig? Flowery
Glenkinchie? Warming Linkwood? Rough edged Glen
Garioch? Unctious Balvenie?

I sit here with the Gold Medal of old age, in a warm, tight
room walled with books and over my head a loft stuffed
with more books. It has been a good day and now I am
tired. Tomorrow can take care of itself when it arrives.

        a glass of whisky
        with a wee drop of water
        at the day's ending

Beginnings

In 1948 our family moved out of a tenement close in Edinburgh's Tollcross area in the city centre to the brand new post-war housing estate of Colinton Mains. The houses had been built by a private developer for the City Council, but had been rejected because of inadequate soundproofing between floors, and because the inside staircases were too steep. Some had been sold; most, like ours, were rented. They were four in a block, two up, two down, and we had an upstairs house, with a view overlooking the outbuildings of Oxgangs Farm. This was then the city's outer periphery; beyond our houses there were open fields as far as the foot of the Pentland Hills. It was an ideal environment for a young family to grow up in. I was six. I could do anything.

Surrounded by young families it was natural and easy for my brother and I to make friends with children from the neighbouring houses. Equally, our parents expanded their circle of friends, and the place became a community. But it was a community without a centre. There was no school, there were only a handful of shops, and the doctor's surgery was in his home, a somewhat larger bungalow—a bought hoose—nearby. A church, for those who appreciated such things, was built later.

I had started my schooling at Tollcross Primary, but Colinton Mains was outside its catchment area. Our nearest school was Craiglockhart Primary, closer to the Slateford area. Transport was a problem, then as now. There was no bus service to the outlying areas, so every day a gaggle of schoolchildren would walk up to Firhill, near the army barracks, and catch the 27 tram. One of my teachers, and I forget how old I was when I met him, was Mr MacCaig. That's how we knew him. Norman came much later.

But we were here, out in the country, or as near as, and that was all that mattered. In the farmyard, through the green-painted iron railings which separated our back garden from it, was a pine tree with a horizontal bough on which, it was said, Robert

Louis Stevenson used to sit. It was, in truth, quite close to his home at Swanston. We used to pass his house on our gang's frequent expeditions into the hills, boys and girls together, with no supervision. After Swanston Farm, our path led alongside a golf course, until we reached the 'T' Woods. This was a little decorative plantation of pines on top of a small hillock. From whichever direction you approached it, the trees formed the shape of the letter T. In reality, the arms formed a cross, still do, but we couldn't see that from ground level. Then we were climbing the slopes of Caerketton, skirting the crag below the summit until we reached the heathery top, and with the vistas of the whole Pentland range in front of us. And there we would play, as children do, unaware of the passing hours and the possible concerns of parents, until the sun began to set. If there is a Heaven, that is where it will be.

> a concrete playground
> the big school in the city
> freedom in the hills

Growing

I've always grown things—flowers, cacti, trees, fruit and vegetables—and growing food crops gives me the most tangible satisfaction. I love to eat what I grow.

Our garden in Dunbar is quite small; too small to grow the quantity and variety of produce we need. I put my name down on the list for Council allotments, but with no new sites being acquired it was a bit of a forlorn hope. After five years I had climbed up the list, but I could see no prospect of getting a Council allotment in the foreseeable future.

Then a friend of mine told me of an idea he'd had for private allotments on land owned by a farmer he knew. This triangular parcel of ground had been cut off from the rest of the farm by a new road development. It was too small to cultivate, and had been left lying fallow, apart from a large barn erected at one end. First a plough and stone-picker went over the ground, piling up the stones in three windrows dividing the field. We used these as the basis for our first paths. We paced the land and marked out a series of 120m² plots, then started advertising them to those on the Council waiting list and beyond. The farmer put in rabbit-proof fencing and a water supply. My friend overcame the Stalinist central planning mindset of East Lothian's planners, and we now have 46 plots on the site, enthusiastically cultivated by a wide variety of growers.

My plot is divided into quarters for ease of crop rotation, further subdivided to make practical beds. One quarter houses the fruit cage, compost bin and shed—all growers need a shed. On the others I plant brassicas, onions, beans, potatoes and root crops. I have three apple trees—two dessert varieties and one for cooking—and a young damson bush.

It's hugely satisfying to pick the first ripe pea pod every year, to shell it, and to taste the sweet and tender peas. With potatoes you can't tell what's happening below ground; you just have to hope for a good crop. With everything else you can see what you're going to get. The main harvest is now in, and I've got onions drying in the shed, three sacks of potatoes for the months ahead, and the freezer full of peas, haricot beans, broad beans, and currants to make jelly.

The gooseberry jam was delicious, thank you for asking. Sorry I couldn't leave you any.

> there's a lot of good
> in digging, as your man wrote
> a lot meant hard work

Harlow Carr

I visit Harlow Carr in the off-season, when the colourful wonders
of summer are not yet visible. It is a reconnaissance trip for an
environmental art project, so coming here in early spring is
better—I can see the structure of the garden and its possibilities
much easier than if I came later. I love gardens when they are
full of happy visitors enjoying themselves, but they would be
a distraction today; this is work! But such enjoyable work.

A tall birch fans out branches and twigs from its papery white trunk;
two crows below it are quartering the lawn for grubs and worms. The
path snakes between winter-colouring shrubs to the stream. Alder
prefer these moist margins, their exposed roots showing pink nodules
where nitrogen is fixed into nutrients to feed the spring shoots.

Into the woodland, past heaps of sawn logs carved in the shapes
of mushrooms, artists have constructed airy sculptural objects
from woven willow. Willow branches—withies or wands—are
useful and attractive, easy to bend into graceful curving shapes
or utilitarian and equally beautiful objects like baskets, fences,
chairs. At this time of year the birds are setting up their three-
dimensional territories. It's relatively easy to outline out on a flat
map the territories of terrestrial creatures, but birds have the
additional freedom of height. Polypore fungi have left black scabs
on the birch trunk. A hemlock grove looks well between beeches
holding onto their dead leaves throughout a rustling winter.
On either side of a hemlock twig the flat needles are of uneven
lengths. Their Latin specific name, *heterophylla*, reflects this.

Doric columns from the old spa frame a view of a shelter belt, home
to rooks whose calls fail to bully the little birds at the feeding station.
I look through the chained field glasses at brilliant bullfinch, quick
flitting long-tails, a robin on the ground evading a hungry squirrel.

The log maze doesn't present much of a challenge—I make
one wrong turn, but getting out is just left, left, right and

left. In the upper branches of trees algae shines bright green, especially when wet. Oak's gnarly bark contrasts with the smoothness of beech—the 'Buch' of the woodland.

Dark, smooth and spiky, holly's waxed leaves stay on, but the berries don't last much beyond Christmas. Blackbirds and thrushes usually polish them off. A hawthorn retains a few wrinkling berries left behind by waxwings and fieldfares. The garden's in the hungry gap.

> before daffodils
> the garden's structure's clear but
> birds don't need the paths

Aipples

Two winters ago I planted three apple trees on my allotment—two eating apples and a Bramley—there's no apple better than a Bramley for baking pies or puddings. Last spring they flowered, but I took off all the tiny fruits right away, to make the trees put their energies into building strong roots and healthy stems. Apple blossom is beautiful; the outsides of the petals are pink to begin with, then they fade to white when fully open. Faint lines inside them glow brightly in UV light, guiding bees to the nectar at their centres. The trees are braced diagonally, with short stakes, which through time makes the trunk thicker, sturdy enough to withstand the strong winds blowing from all points of the compass.

This spring the dessert varieties flowered early, both at the same time, and pollination was very good. I let them set fruit. The Bramley flowered briefly, but much later, and didn't set at all. After the usual 'June drop' when excess fruits are shed naturally, I went over the trees again, taking off the smallest baby apples, and thinning the biggest fruit clusters. I was left with a dozen apples on each tree.

July came and went, a truly beautiful month, as was August. The apples began to swell and to take on colour. By early September the 'Discovery' apples were beautiful: bright red, glossy and very large. They would be ripe by the end of the month. The other variety, Red Devil, had even larger fruit, far bigger than any apple I've seen in shops, and a deeper red, the colour more evenly distributed over the satin gloss skin. These take longer to ripen, and would be ready by the end of October. Their flesh is pink-tinged and tastes of strawberries.

And then, visiting the allotment one Sunday morning after a week on the road, I discovered someone had taken half the Red Devil fruit, although they were nowhere near ripe. I was sure Discovery would make up for it. The tree looked gorgeous, and was much admired by my fellow growers. A week later I found nine of its apples had been stolen, leaving me with only three fruits.

It wasn't just Adam and Eve who stole the forbidden fruit. it must surely have been thieves who came in the night, for I couldn't bring myself to suspect anyone from the allotments.

But now my friend Mary has given me her poems in the Doric about the Biblical story, *The Angel and the Aipple*, and I'm thinking again about the knowledge of good and evil, and the serpent of suspicion is slithering into my mind. Lots of my friends at the allotments admired my aipples, but did one of them steal them?

first fruit, nearly ripe
almost ready to harvest
stolen from the trees

Eden

The colours seem truer, more vivid, in the South of France. In sunlight of such intensity, all colours are bright, and all shadows are deeper, darker. The vineyards are an even green hue, from the other side of the Canal du Midi just outside our holiday apartment, to as far as the rising ground of the Corbieres, and the far Pyrenees on the southern horizon. There's a different green from the plane trees edging the River Aude, broken up by the silver undersides of willow leaves. Fallow fields are a paler green, rusted with the reddish flower-heads of a grass common round these parts. In a few weeks, the fields will be a uniform yellow colour, and they'll stay that way until next spring unless they're ploughed. In the hills, the scrubby vegetation seems very dark from a distance—that's the evergreen shrubs of the garrigue—and there's a pastel mottling from the herbage, where mauves, purples and blues predominate. There's an occasional exclamation of yellow, some silver, and rare reds.

Walking along the road inland from the Canal we look at the plants growing along the roadside; some are familiar, others new to us. As usual, from my time working at the Royal Botanic Garden Edinburgh, I try to name them. But that was part of another world where such things were important, were of the nature of the institution and its work. Suddenly we come across a dead snake, which has failed to out-slither an anonymous car on its way across the road. It's a recent road-kill, still oozing blood from a broken mouth and everted anus. Another hour on that road, in that heat, and it will be too dry to feed kite or magpie. Two hours and it will be a belt.

At sunset the cicadas make their chirping noise in the trees, and down by the Canal the evening bullfrogs clear their throats and start their chorus. The late laugh of a woodpecker somewhere in the pine woods provides more sound effects as the light begins to fade. On the other side of the waterway, a field of ripening melons goes from brilliant gold to pale yellow, then loses colour completely. It's time to open a bottle of local red wine and reflect on the content of the day.

forgotten a hat
Languedoc summer sunshine
bakes a northern brain

Wrongs

I get depressed when I think about some of the things going on in the world. To anyone who knows anything about science, it's clear beyond any reasonable doubt that human activities are affecting the world's climate, but some clownish politicians still argue against it, for reasons more to do with ego, greed or ignorance than any rational consideration of the facts or concern for future generations. And yet these bastards are the only ones who can put changes into effect.

Shrinking biodiversity is happening here and now to some extent, but it's much more worrying in tropical habitats, where rainforest trees are cut down by unscrupulous logging companies, and natural forest is cleared to grow palm oil trees to feed our insatiable demands for detergents and vegetable oils. And it's not just the loss of trees, but the loss of the plant, animal and bird communities which depend on them, that should concern us.

We're losing our bees because farmers have financial incentives to use toxic pesticides to control harmful pests, without considering their effects on beneficial insects. Who's going to pollinate our food crops when the bees are extinct? Politicians'? I think not. And what about the birds which depend on the insects. Are MPs and MSPs going to sing in the fields to make up for their losses? I doubt it. When politicians try the solfa scale they never get any higher than Mi Mi Mi.

When are we going to stop littering our coasts and seas with plastic? On my local beach I often come across dead seabirds strangled with the blue twine used by the fishermen and discarded overboard. And at the other end of the scale, whales have been found drowned, tangled in creel lines just offshore. And for what? To feed diners in Spanish restaurants. Crazy.

At times I must admit to having a sneaking liking for Kenny Everett's 'Mr Angry' and his splenetic rages, although I couldn't always agree with his choice of targets.

I think it's maybe Zen that has kept me calm most of the time. I still hate injustice, unfairness, intolerance, prejudice, racism, sexism, militarism, bigotry and extreme nationalism, but sometimes it's hard to believe you can take action to defeat all these evils.

Hamlet said it all, really

Last of Japan

From our Hakone hotel window an early view of Fuji-san
changing colour as the sun rises. On the other side Lake
Ashi, reflecting the mountain in its mirror.

To Owakudane, the Valley of Great Boiling, for views of fumaroles,
boiling springs, a cable car and a geothermal energy plant. There's
a cable between the hotel and one of the springs, and baskets of
eggs are sent up on the wire to be boiled, then sent back down to
the restaurant for sale. The eggshells turn black from the hydrogen
sulphide in the water, and we are not tempted to try them. The whole
hillside is punctured by hissing vents, wreathed in steam, and the
water in the springs smells terrible. But it's sensible to make use of
this natural source of energy in a country lacking in fossil fuels.
This region reminds me of Iceland, but without the Blue Lagoon.

We have a sail on Lake Ashi, admiring a passing paddle steamer
and the orange torii gate on the landing stage, before driving
down to the coast on the final leg of our trip. This part of the
road is on the old *Kisokaido*, one of two routes linking Tokyo
and Kyoto, and is lined with spectacular *Cryptomeria* trees.

Kamakura is the site of a famous temple with a huge bronze statue
of the seated Amida Buddha. His head is a separate casting, resting
on a free-standing pillar within the hollow body. This way, if
there's an earthquake, he may shake his head, but it won't fall off.

Back in Tokyo we buy *o-bento* boxes in a department store
and take them back to our hotel. We put on our *yukata*
robes and eat our meal watching a *kendo* match on TV.

Flying home next day, we chase the terminator across
the roof of the world.

itte kimasu	I go but will return
domo arigato, gozaimasu	thank you very much
oyasuminasai	goodnight

Homage

Paintings don't just tell you about their subjects—people, landscapes, birds, beasts, flowers—they tell you about the artists themselves, their worlds, their times, their choices. Going to galleries is always interesting, even if you know the place and its contents well. Almost always I find something I hadn't noticed before.

So visiting a gallery new to me, in an unfamiliar city, is even more exciting. I'll never forget our visit to the Hermitage in St Petersburg, or to the galleries in Dresden and Frankfurt. The Prado in Madrid is one of the world's great galleries, housing 3,000 paintings, the possessions of the Spanish Royal Family. We visited it in 2004 with our group of friends, guided by two art historians. Our man, young but very knowledgeable, tells us it is impossible to see everything in the time we have, but wants us to concentrate on just five paintings. This seems to be an admirable approach, so we set off, but in the course of walking round, I naturally see other paintings I would like to spend time studying on a return visit. A portrait of Mary Tudor by Sir Anthony More, for instance, is one I've seen many times in history books, but never the original. She seems even more stern, but even more human, here and in close up. I have to confess I'm distracted by it, and I don't pay attention to what he's saying about the portrait of Philip II by Rubens.

> representations
> of dead kings and queens look out
> at future subjects

But then we come to Hieronymus Bosch: *The Garden of Earthly Delights*. It's a triptych, showing Heaven, Hell and the in-between. Hell, of course, is the most interesting of the three, populated by grotesque, malevolent imaginary creatures doing vile things to suffering human beings—no more than they deserve, I expect. The El Greco is not as interesting as one we would see later in a church in Toledo—*The Burial of the Count of Orgaz*; but the Goyas are terrific, from the Majas, clothed and naked, to the infamous Black Paintings, including Saturn eating his child, a very disturbing image. The 3rd of May painting is vivid and thought-provoking. But the huge Velázquez painting, *Las Meninas*, is my highlight. We see here the Spanish royals, the King and Queen in the background, cousins of course, and the beautiful, doomed little princess in the foreground, surrounded by her attendants and playmates. We see the artist himself, proud, distinguished, adorned with the insignia of an honour bestowed on him by the king.

Some years later, visiting Barcelona, we visited the Museu Picasso, and were taken aback by the room devoted to the artist's interpretations of Las Meninas. Here again we have the Princess, her attendants, the King and Queen, Velazquez himself, interpreted in completely different ways, by a master of 20th century painting, like a jazz musician improvising on a riff. It's not all that different from a writer viewing a painting then composing a poem inspired by it. Like Picasso, we writers can attempt to interpret the subject and to show how it makes us feel. I know some critics don't approve of ekphrastic poetry but art is as valid a subject for poetry as any other.

> in the gallery
> paintings escape from the walls
> and into our minds

Wiener Blut

Off Porzellanstrasse we come upon a Bierkeller named 'Centimeter'. Forty Scottish friends pile into the big room downstairs and look at the menu, which is printed and folded to resemble a ruler, metric of course. We discover they sell beer in Zapfsäule, which translates as 'Petrol Pumps', and since it sounds like an economy of scale to canny Scots, we order up our first 5-litre container. After some time it arrives, and is placed on a central table. It stands about half a metre high, and has a tap near the bottom where we fill our glasses. Since it has taken a while to pour, and is very popular with our party, we immediately order another two, and begin to enjoy ourselves as old Scottish friends on the loose in foreign cities tend to do. We talk loudly, sing Scottish songs and then local songs, in this case Viennese ones. The words seem to get lost somewhere around the end of the first verse, and from then on it is all *la-la*. Still, I believe we gave our hosts some colourful insights into the Scottish character. I think they enjoyed it. We certainly did.

Next day we have a tour of the Schönbrun Palace, monumental and very beautiful. To my chagrin, our guide, while extolling the virtues of the Empress Maria Theresa and her success in producing marriageable children to cement international alliances, fails to mention that she had a wonderful collection of exotic plants. Their Keeper, Nicholaus Jacquin, commissioned the brilliant Bauer brothers to paint several hundred of them for a magnificent four-volume set of books, a copy of which I am familiar with from the Royal Botanic Garden Edinburgh's library. (Did I mention that I used to be the librarian?)

We stop for lunch after our walking tour of the city, and I have a local rustic speciality, Blunzengröstl. It's made from black pudding and sliced potatoes, with onions and spices. So that's the Blut bit. It was delicious.

The architecture of Vienna is varied and wonderful, from the majestic and formal through the rococo to Art Nouveau. And the

Hundertwasser Haus was just round the corner from our hotel.

We have a Heurigen evening in Grinzing, with entertainment from professional singers and dancers. I have to say however, that the Austrian 'new' wine wasn't a centimetre off passing for battery acid. I'd rather have had the beer, but it wasn't on offer.

> 25 litres of beer
> went down far too easily
> said the Student Prince

Danube Blues

We drive from Vienna to Budapest, not a long journey, but it crosses a border between countries with many differences in histories, cultures and languages. I've got my own memories of the Hungarian Uprising in 1956, seeing newsreel footage of Soviet tanks in the streets. It was the time, back home, when the unreconstructed Scottish poet Hugh MacDiarmid joined the Communist Party, in a very public gesture of support for Russia. That's maybe coloured my views on him and his nationalism ever since. I remember Imre Nagy being executed, and the 'Goulash Communism' of the Kadar regime which followed. Hungary has always been different. It was pro-German at the start of the Second World War, no doubt hoping to regain territory lost to Romania, Serbia and Slovakia following the break-up of the Austro-Hungarian Empire. It had ended up being occupied by Germany and ruled by a puppet Nazi regime until 'liberation' by the Red Army. All in the past. What would the country be like now, I wondered. Hard to tell from a motorway. I mean, who could guess what Tranent is like from a bus on the A1? At the time we visit in 2002, the country is about to join the EU, and is eager to welcome tourists.

On the outskirts of the city, we pass through hilly country— lightly forested limestone scarps, a patchwork of autumn colours, smallholdings, dachas, out-of-town shopping malls, like Barstow or the Gateshead Metro Centre. We walk down the main street—Vàci Utca—and reach the Danube, not looking particularly blue under a grey sky. We cross the famous Chain Bridge, built by the Scottish engineer Adam Clark.

Hero Square has twin curved colonnades with statues of major figures from Hungary's past, from Arpad to Kossuth. The Central Market is very impressive, with stalls selling absolutely everything. We see some of the locals buying pig-related comestibles; pig's heads, pig's other bits, squeals and sausages. The goulash soup is excellent, and the restaurant is, thankfully, violin-free, a luxury in Budapest.

On our final full day in the city, the two of us take the Metro then walk up Gellert Hill, named after a martyred priest who was rolled down it in a barrel, to the Citadel. On the path up the hill we are approached by one of a group of four unsavoury-looking characters, but we make a detour and give him the slip. He may have just wanted a light for his cigarette, but I rather doubt it. Most of the time, travelling in many different countries and cities, I feel safe. In most of Budapest I felt safe, but here I was uneasy. At the top of the hill, the Liberation Monument is huge, crude, very Soviet in style, and heavily graffitied in a variety of languages. The F word is fairly universal though. But the view from the top, over Buda, Pest and the dividing Danube, is very fine.

We are unable to avoid the 'gypsy' entertainment in the restaurant that night. It's not my favourite Hungarian music by a long shot. I'm fond of Bartok and Kodaly, but this is neither. Czardaš with your goulash, sir?

> the old Red poet
> spoke up for old tyrannies
> from his Brownsbank home

House of cards

After my mother died I contacted the lawyer who had been dealing with her affairs, and he agreed to handle the winding up of her estate and the sale of her house. My brother and I were executors, and neither of us wanted to buy the house ourselves. He was living temporarily in Switzerland, and would shortly return to America. I didn't want a second home, albeit a nice house in a very nice village in an attractive part of rural Perthshire. It just wouldn't be practical for the occasional use we might make of it.

When you live to be 92, even with a very modest income, it's all too easy to accumulate things—furniture, clothing, fabrics, ornaments, photographs (Oh God, the photographs!), pictures, kitchenware, things you can't remember why you bought, bric-a-brac—in short, *stuff*. So there was an awful lot of work involved in clearing the house, all too many visits to the charity shops and the Council recycling depot.

My mother had been certain that her furniture was valuable, and would form part of a reasonable legacy for my brother and I. I wasn't so sure, so I called in a local auction house valuer. 'You couldn't give it away' was his considered opinion. In the end I had to pay to have her furniture cleared. She would have been heartbroken.

And the house itself was not the asset it might have been. Some time before my father died he had taken out a loan against it, and coerced my mother into signing the papers (this was the cause of our final estrangement) for some kind of equity release scam dreamt up by corrupt lawyers and grasping bankers, under which they would gain three-quarters of any appreciation in value of the house between the loan date and the eventual sale of the house. So my brother and I never expected much of a financial legacy—I always thought *we* were our parents' legacy.

And then, last December, just before the house was due to be sold, a pipe burst in the loft, flooding the house for several days in the interval between inspection visits. It caused irrecoverable damage to ceilings, floors, internal walls and plasterwork. They all had to be stripped out and dried, leaving a shell. And the insurance company, another bunch of crooks, wouldn't pay out, as the house was unoccupied.

But today, at last, the house has been sold, albeit at a much lower price than everyone estimated. The only consolation is that the greedy bastards in the bank won't make anything like the amount they were expecting. But I still feel cheated by them and the crooked lawyer who persuaded my father to sign up to the deal.

> it's a true saying
> what's for ye'll no go by ye
> unlucky for some

Luna

It's always been there, well it's been there all my life, so that's almost the same as always, isn't it? As a child and as a man I've never had the slightest desire to go there, but I'm very pleased that other people did. I was energised by Kennedy's inaugural, as so many others were. That brought it from a dream to a distinct possibility, and then a reality, that men would, 'before the decade is out' walk on the surface of that silvery globe. And they have all been men; surely that can't be right?

Back in July 1969 we came home early from a holiday just so that we could watch the landing live on television. I remember the grainy footage and the crackly sound of 'one small step'. I watched the return, and then the next one. Then came Apollo 13 and the near 'Disaster in Space'. I was enthralled, fearful and relieved by turns. And I watched all the others until 17, the last one, with geologist Harrison 'Jack' Schmitt on board. By then I was trained in geology and got to hear him speak at a lecture in Edinburgh.

New Moon, Old Moon, how do you tell the difference? Well, in the Moon's first phase, after it peeps out behind our shadow, the right-hand limb is the first to be illuminated by the Sun, so there's a right-hand crescent. The easiest way to remember it is to write a capital N with the down stroke curved, like). It can be written to look like NEW. The old moon's a left-hand crescent, so it starts with (for OLD. Simples.

What the astronauts brought back—Moon rocks—told a very interesting and unexpected story about the origin of the Earth-Moon system. The Moon is by far the largest satellite, relative to its planet, in the Solar System. The conjecture had been that it was a 'wanderer', captured by the pull of Earth's gravity. If that were so, we would expect its bulk composition to be different from Earth's, because its minerals would have had a different history. It doesn't; it matches ours to several decimal points for most elements. So we must have been one body at one time. The current explanation is that a Mars-sized body collided with Earth in the Solar System's early days, and the ejecta coalesced through gravity to assemble the Moon. But it was a very different place; molten, and very close to Earth, until its angular momentum moved it away very gradually. It's still moving away, at around an inch and a half every year. But it's part of us, and always has been.

giant steps
for all mankind
walking on the Earth

Mines

I lie in the lee of the wall and imagine the spring sunshine holds
the warmth of an approaching summer. The breeze, which is
fairly constant in the Bathgate Hills, makes ripples in the grass,
carries the sounds of growing lambs, but lifts over the wall
without cooling me. I sleep for a while, aware of dreaming, but
forgetting the dream's content when I wake up. Why is it some
dreams are memorable, but others not? Memories are the same.
And confusing dreams for memories is not a good idea.

A dry-stane dyke circles the crown of trees on the hillock, for no
apparent reason. Fields slope up from the road towards it, mostly hay
on the slope, with ploughed fields on the flatter ground closer to the
farmhouse. Set into the hillside there's a locked iron gate, its bars too
close-set to squeeze through. Looking through it, I sense only the
dripping darkness and the depths of the mine. Coffin levels, that's
what they call this type of mining—where the profile of the mine level
is shaped for minimum access, one person at a time. Head and feet
are narrow, take less space, less rock to remove; broader at shoulder
height. A great place for bats, which hibernate here in winter.

Was there a fox? High sun, long grass blowing, cloud-shadows
passing quickly, and I'm sure I remember a fox, running up
the hill, sniffing, seeking anything edible, looking back at
me watching; tail fluffed up and straight out behind it.

The Hillhouse Mine is easy to explore, a choice of four or five
ways in, but the slope is very steep. A hard slope to pull stone out,
but they rigged up endless belts, hooked on the wooden sleds,
and used horses to walk round a pulley wheel, hauling up the
full loads, letting the empties slide down into the candlelight. No
gases here, quarrying into the hillside had opened the whole mine
to the air. In the depths of the mine there's a kiln, so some of the
stone was burnt below ground to make lime. The roof is a massive
sandstone, supported on big pillars of limestone. Safe, mostly, but
when it does fall, the bits that come down are massive. Killers.

The Silver Mine is near Hilderston. A group of us, all young
geologists, explored Aitken's 1919 adit, putting in a drain through
a rockfall. Light from the entrance glinted in a little way, and
our breath steamed in the cold air. The floor was wet, running
in a little stream toward the entrance. The roof was supported
by timbers, but they were rotted. I squeezed the water out
of one piece, like a sponge. We never did find any silver ore,
but on a side vein at the surface we found heavy pink barites,
and galena—lead ore. An 18th century map of the area shows
several mineshafts, with names like 'The White Hole' 'The Gin
Sink' (where the pumping en*gine* sat), and 'God's Blessing'.

I walk back down to the car, the wind now blowing through
my hair. As I pass a blackthorn thicket I smell the distinctive
odour of fox. I turn and look back up the hill, but the
only thing moving there now is the rippling grass.

> going underground
> to find the hidden treasure
> dreams and memories

Cathar country

We are based in a small village, Paraza, on the banks of the
Canal du Midi, in the Languedoc region. It is swelteringly hot
when we arrive, but quite cool inside our holiday home, a tiny,
3-storey building with a roof terrasse overlooking the Canal.

It's a good base for exploring. I'm intrigued by the story of
the Cathars, the Albigensian Crusade and the troubled times
of the 13th century. I want to know more about the people of
that place, why they were hunted down and persecuted, and
why their faith was so strong that they would die for it.

We visit Carcassonne first, as do most tourists. The old Cité is
interesting, but much of it is a highly imaginative 19th century
reconstruction. Beziers is a pleasant town, but not really
medieval—it too has been modernised, and there's no trace of
the massacre of 1209, when the besieging Crusaders, under the
control of the Papal legate, Arnold-Amaury, asked how they would
recognise the Cathar heretics? 'Kill them all,' he said, 'the Lord
will know which are His.' So they did, as many as 12,000 men,
women and children, in the name of the Church and its beliefs.

The Cathar castles, the ones which remain, are perched on top
of high mountain peaks in this rugged limestone country. We
park below the castle of Queribus, and walk up the steep path to
its impressive walls. It's a strong fortress and, standing where the
defenders would have stood, it's clear it could withstand a prolonged
siege. Peyrepertuse is my favourite of the Cathar *bastides*. Strung
out along a ridge at the head of a vertiginous road, the views from
its ramparts take in the whole of the Ariege, the Montagnes Noires,
the Corbieres and the distant Pyrenees. It was besieged, but the
attackers scaled the near-vertical cliffs and forced an entrance.

Minerve is, to me, the most poignant of the Cathar strongholds. Here
the army, by now under the command of Simon de Montfort (no,
not that one), laid siege. The town is built on a rocky promontory

overlooking a gorge, which is dry most of the year, and a huge cave, into which the winter river flows. A replica of a trebuchet, a siege engine, stands now where the real one, named 'Bad Neighbour', stood in 1210. It delivered such a battering to the town that its precious and essential water cistern was destroyed. The townspeople had no choice; they gave up their Cathars, and 140 were burned to death in the dry river bed. After the burning they shovelled mud over the corpses so the stench wouldn't offend the Crusader army.

Some of my questions have been answered, but the visit has given me the impetus to learn more, and to speak about it.

> bright bee-eaters flash
> over the willowed water
> pleasure boats sail by

A sense of balance

I have two bikes at home. One is a hybrid bike I use for day-to-day activities, cycling to the gym, for light shopping, and for short, local journeys. It's got all-terrain tyres, so I can take it off-road, along the dunes from the Barns Ness lighthouse to Skateraw for example. That's a very pleasant run on a nice day, with lots to see along the way. It's not a true mountain bike; it doesn't have the suspension system or the gears needed to ride it comfortably on hill and forest tracks, but it's fine otherwise.

The other one is a road bike, a lightweight one with dropped handlebars. It's built for speed, and it really does shift. The frame is made from aluminium alloy—I can lift it with one hand. The problem, if there is one, is with the pedals. The ones it came with can either take cleated cycling shoes or toe-clips. I've never used cleats in the past, and the idea of my feet being locked in to pedals is a bit scary. I suppose I could practise releasing my feet, but I haven't done that. Mostly, I use the toe-clips.

One day at the beginning of summer I got the bike out and made it ready for the season. Then I set off for a short run. The sea mist—haar—was down, but it wasn't particularly thick, and promised to burn off later. I would cycle to White Sands, past the giant hole in the ground left after Lafarge closed this section of quarry.

I was on the cycle track which parallels the road, and coming rapidly downhill to the point where the track joins the road. It's a right-angle turn, but I can usually cut the corner if I'm not going too fast. But as I approached I noticed a car coming down the hill, and I estimated we would both reach the junction simultaneously. So I tried to brake and turn at the same time. I flew over the handlebars; my feet, trapped in the toe-clips, whipped my body round, and I landed heavily on my wrist. It hurt, so I swore quite creatively—I find that helps against pain—but I knew it was broken; a hand shouldn't be at that angle to its arm. It turned out to be a Smith's fracture of the radius, requiring an operation and the permanent insertion of a steel plate in my arm. But it hasn't put me off cycling. Ride on, Syd Barrett, ride on.

> I've got a bike it's
> very very fast in fact
> so fast it scares me

Dark water, deep dips

Loch Lubnaig is my favourite Scottish loch. It's a narrow one,
filling a deep glen between mountains on either side, twisting
and turning, following the route of a long gone glacier. Its waters
are dark, shaded by the hills, but I've never found it gloomy.

The road which winds alongside it is a favourite one for motorcycling,
full of dips and rises, sharp bends and a few open straights, the
riding thrills bikers enjoy. I used to love it on my small Honda
185, but other guys on bigger bikes always passed me, roaring
along the highway, leaning into the bends, overtaking and then
cutting in. Sadly, little bunches of plastic-wrapped flowers along
the road testify to the fact that some of them don't make it to the
end of the road. I can't deny the appeal of biking, because I loved
it too, but I always knew it wasn't the safest mode of transport.

I used to think pedal bikes were safer, and so they are, mostly, but
not always. I was driving to Comrie one sunny summer Sunday
morning to stay with my mother so I could take her for a hospital
appointment the following day, taking the back road through the
hills, another favourite route. You could reliably predict seeing lots of
wildlife on this road, and I often did—mountain hares, a blackcock
lek, a short-eared owl hunting in daylight as they do, red kites, hen
harriers. There is always something to see here. Today, looking ahead,
I see a peloton of cyclists, around 30 or 40 of them, obviously out
for a club run. The group, cycling four abreast, is far too large for
me to overtake safely on this narrow, steep and winding road, but
I'm not in a hurry; there's plenty of time to admire the road and the
mountains. The weather is beautiful, and I am very relaxed. There's
another driver in front of me and we both hold back so as not to
crowd the cyclists, who are doing a fair lick of speed downhill.

Then they reach the flat ground at the foot of the hills, the floodplain
on which Comrie is built. And they start to race each other, weaving
and wobbling. Suddenly I see bikes at the front of the group fly into
the air. When I reach the melee I find one cyclist slightly injured, but

another lying stretched out, deeply unconscious. The paramedics are called, and, on advice from another cyclist, a GP, the Air Ambulance helicopter, which lands in the field near the crash. I give what comfort I can to the other cyclists, but, listening to the distinctive and horrible breathing sounds of the injured man, there is nothing anyone can do for him. He died in hospital a few hours later, according to the police.

fair weather cycling
travelling at break-neck speeds
until the last stop

And miles to go

I'm going through a period of insomnia just now. I go to bed maybe an hour earlier than I would at home but I'm tired earlier. I haven't been doing anything strenuous during the day—no gym, no digging—but I can't keep my eyes open.

And I fall asleep almost immediately, but wake up at 4.30, sometimes 3.30, and I can't get back to sleep again. I can't figure out the reason for it, so I lie awake worrying about it. And it doesn't make sense to worry, because that just keeps me awake.

It's something that never happened to me when I was working, when I had to be wide awake and alert, eager to absorb information, to take decisions, to get things done. These pressures are off me now. Though I may sometimes have dreams about my old career, it's in the past, a long way in the past.

I'm pretty sure it's nothing physical; my health is good and my metabolism is stable. I haven't been over-eating or drinking to excess—a couple of glasses of wine with a meal isn't excessive. I've read that this pattern of insomnia is a sign of depression, but I don't feel depressed. Can you be depressed without knowing it? I'm happy, life is going well, and at the moment I have no major problems to deal with; quite the reverse, in fact.

Maybe it's a release from previous tensions, an absence of outstanding commitments, a lack of deadlines, that's made my subconscious think it's time to give me a bit of a jolt, a wake-up call? Do I worry because I have no worries? Fuck. It's enough to make a person depressed. I'll sleep on it. Or maybe not.

> mistaking the time
> on the hands of the clock
> four hours until dawn

The way of Zen

By nature I'm an independent cuss; if I can do things my own way I will, and the same applies to my Zen practice. Meditation is at the heart of it. I have never had any desire to join with others, sitting cross-legged in a temple, chanting or staying silent; sitting just to sit (*zazen*) or contemplating philosophical riddles (*koan*) to which there are no rational correct answers.

Even if my arthritic knees and stiff joints would permit (and increasingly they won't), I see no point in sitting cross-legged: one posture is as good as any other, and there's no specific advantage to body or mind in any of them. And my Zen practice is my Zen practice and nobody else's, and doesn't have to be a communal thing. I see no point in that either. I have nothing against those whose practice differs from mine. And I have absolutely no desire to proselytize, to convert others to think as I do. That would be insufferably rude and unspeakably arrogant. (Door-to-door evangelists please note).

I practice meditation through action. Running, cycling, walking, hill-walking, digging or working out at the gym; these are among the many ways I can enter the state of 'no mind' which leads to moments of enlightenment.

> sitting about
> to no great purpose
> makes the place untidy

Circus

It is my birthday—a gloriously warm and sunny July day. In the morning we travel to the big shop in the square, to buy some things for the evening party. We are out on our own for this expedition, trusted to find our way there, and to return safely. We feel only slightly apprehensive, after all, I can read the names of the streets and the underground stations.

We come back with our little purchases, stow them safely away, and meet up with our friends for an afternoon excursion to the circus. At home a trip to the circus wouldn't normally be a big attraction, but I'm on holiday, it *is* my birthday and I am determined to enjoy it. We drive there in a large bus, going round some of the nicer parts of the city, and then we arrive.

Our seats are high in the vast arena, but not too high—these are not the cheapest seats. We look around at a sea of faces, and down to the double ring where the acts will perform. The lights dim, the Ringmaster comes out and says some things I don't understand, and the show begins.

I am utterly entranced by the spectacle, and wrapped up in the whole experience. The band is excellent, the trapeze artists glamorous and daring, the clowns mime uproariously, bareback riders show their skills on horses whose backsides glow like polished chestnuts, and the jugglers perform feats I've never seen before. But it's the animals that surprise me most. Trained elephants and lions are familiar beasts in British circuses at that time, but I've never seen a polar bear in the ring, albeit a muzzled one, and I never imagined I'd watch a vulture riding on the back of a tiger, parading round on a leash.

Amazed and exhilarated, we catch our bus back to the hotel Cosmos, where I open the champagne I bought that morning in GUM on Red Square. We get royally pissed. After all, it isn't every day that a man turns 40, and gets the chance to see the Moscow State Circus—in Moscow.

two rings
one spectacle
life's a circus

All about books

For most of my working life I was a librarian, with the exception of a few years early on when I was a beatnik barman, and the latter years when I've become an author and publisher. I started off in public libraries in West Lothian. But I had always been interested in science, and I wanted to work in scientific libraries, so when the Open University started in 1971 I was one of its first students. After two years I was one of its first batch of graduates, with a degree in maths and science.

I had qualified in geology and geochemistry, so when a vacancy arose in the then Institute of Geological Sciences (now British Geological Survey) in Edinburgh, I applied and was successful. My first task was to plan the move of the library from its old home in Grange Terrace to a brand new building, Murchison House. Several thousand books, scientific journals and maps had to be accommodated in the new library, and making sure everything moved in the right order to the right places wasn't straightforward.

The main duties in the new library were to provide and manage the research material needed by the scientific staff, and also to provide access to geological maps and other material to the general public. While published geological maps covered relatively large areas at scales down to 1:50,000, detailed maps of Scotland are at a scale of 1:10,000—the so-called six-inch maps—and mostly hand-coloured originals. They were and are an incredibly valuable source of information.

I loved the work, and I told my boss that there was only one job I'd leave it for—librarian at the Royal Botanic Garden Edinburgh, one of the world's great botanical libraries. After fifteen years, the desired vacancy came up, and I got the job.

One of the most obvious differences between geology and botany is the proportion of beards cultivated by their practitioners—very high in the former, quite low in the latter. The library contains early printed books, illustrated herbals from the 16th century, a huge geographical range of national floras, the most up-to date scientific texts and journals, and a vast collection of botanical illustrations, not to mention the historical archives going back to the 1680s. By the time I retired I had occupied a number of posts in senior management at the Garden, but my time in the library was the most rewarding.

> ordered shelves of books
> access to information
> communication

O.M.O.

This one, my writer friend and I agreed, would be all about loneliness. You said you'd been lonely at times. I said I had too, but actually I was lying so that I could appear to share your feelings. It wasn't true. I've been alone often, even in company, but I've never felt loneliness.

Say I'm climbing a mountain, maybe in the Perthshire hills. I could tell you which one I'm remembering, but it wouldn't mean anything to you. I get up early, make my breakfast, prepare my lunch, pack the day-sack, and drive. It's well over a hundred miles from home. I have the radio on—Classic FM, or Radio Two until I feel guilty about listening to crap and switch back, trying to ignore the adverts. I park the car in the public car park outside the village, and set off up the single-track road that leads to a farm set in the hills. That beautiful river that I told you about flows among the conglomerate boulders about 100 yards below the farmhouse. A great spot for a picnic in the summer—sit on the hot rocks and dangle your feet in the pools—but I'm not here for that today. This is serious—I'm here to bag a Munro.

Once I get past the farmhouse, with its chained dog too bored to bark, I'm on a rough track. Over a cattle grid, and I'm right in among the beasts. Most of them are milling round the silage hopper, churning up the glaur. It's early spring, and the grass isn't yet lush enough for grazing at this altitude. They're mostly young winterers, very hairy, and nosy in the way young animals are. A couple of the braver wee stirks try to intimidate me, puffing at the air and stotting their delicate hooves on the ground. I laugh and shake my stick at them, sending them running round behind the others.

Nothing yet about loneliness, you're saying. True, so far I've been among my fellow creatures, close to human habitation, and walking on a metalled road. Let me walk on a bit further then.

I'm at the point where the path heads diagonally up the face of a substantial hill. I look along the track as far as I can see, and there's nobody there; I am truly alone. Except for the sheep, and they don't count. Sheep never count.

I trudge along, gaining height all the time, passing nobody, being passed by nobody, until I reach the shoulder of the hill. I find myself on a long wide ridge that trends upwards over several miles. I see the summit crags (OK, it's Stuc A' Chroin) a long way off, and much higher. I'm the only human being in the landscape. Far below me, on the lower slopes of the next glen, a group of brown boulders resolves into a herd of stags, munching on a new green flush. Their heads are down, but I can see their antlers, not yet dropped. The track winds its way along the whaleback, in and out of eroded peat hags. Meadow pipits flit about in the blow-outs, looking for insects.

Nearly two hours later I'm picking my way through the rock field at the top, heading for the trig point—which I slap—it's my tradition. Knocked the bastard off. I hunker down in the shelter of a house-sized boulder, and eat the sandwiches and fruit I've brought with me. Do I feel lonely? No, I do not. I have spoken to no-one, not even myself, but at no point on the ascent have I felt the slightest twinge of loneliness. On the contrary, I have relished my solitude, my time alone in the mountains. I have never felt the slightest shred of desire to have anyone else with me on these big walks—that would spoil it for me.

So I go back to the point I made at the beginning: I don't know what loneliness is like, because I've never experienced it and I can't imagine it.

So what's your story? Are you lonesome tonight?

> top of the mountain
> not the whole point of the climb—
> only halfway there

Out in the open

There is something very special about reading poetry in the open air, although it has its difficulties. Words can be snatched away by an unruly gust of wind, or drowned out by a passing ambulance. Reading with a wall behind you, or some other solid object, is good for reflecting sound waves back to your listeners. Hedges absorb and diffuse sound, so they don't work so well.

Poems about plants and gardens abound in the literature; many poets find inspiration in the natural world, whether or not they might class themselves as nature poets. Working as I have in public gardens, and knowing and visiting many more, I've taken part in several different types of poetry events in gardens. Poetry walks are very popular, and attract good audiences. To walk in a garden on a spring morning or a summer evening, listening to poems carefully chosen to reflect the beauty of gardens and the joy of gardening, is a lovely experience.

Writing poetry in gardens is something common in Japan, today and in the past. The Japanese court moved regularly from Edo (modern Tokyo) to Kyoto, and to other provincial cities. Courtiers, when not employed on official duties, would come together to socialise and to celebrate. They would paint, make music, or read and write poetry, these being courtly accomplishments essential to while away the idle hours. Composing poetry in a group was the foundation of renga, around the 11th century AD in our version of the calendar. There were rules, and an elaborate system of etiquette. The verses have to link to each other, but in a subtle way. A Master Poet would plan the session and draft a 'schema' to be followed, with the number and order of verses on each subject and so on. A Host Poet would honour the guests, provide the venue, refreshments and copy the verses. Renga, or more fully *haikai-no renga*, developed and became formalised. The verses had to have season words, and be arranged in a defined number of 'sound symbols', the Japanese *onji*. The first verse had lines of five, seven and five onji, the second seven and seven, and so on, alternately. The first verse had to honour the Host and the place, and the second was a reply.

By the time Basho came along in the 17th century, he was popular and highly respected as a renga master. He brought about several significant changes in Japanese literature, mainly by concentrating on the first verse of renga, the hokku. Under his influence, the hokku could develop as a poetic form in its own right, as an independent kind of poem. Since his time, hokku developed into the haiku form we know today. And renga has become popular again in the West.

I've been privileged to take part in many renga over the years, whether as participant, host or master, and some of the best ones have been in gardens—the Hidden Gardens in Glasgow, the Logan and Dawyck gardens, and the Royal Botanic Garden Edinburgh. These, and other gardens, are excellent places for poetry in the open air.

> under the tall trees
> a group of fine poets sits
> let's have some green tea

Old leaves

It's raining again, and the leaves have changed, even in the week
I've been here. The birch leaves have become almost transparent—a
timid suggestion of yellow. And the ash keys that were bright yellow
when I arrived are now brown, and the leaves will all have fallen
by next week. Leaf change is a profound and subtle mechanism;
they shut down their breathing by closing the stomata—the little
openings in the leaf surface—and stop photosynthesis. Nutrients
are transferred downwards for storage in the root systems, leaving
other pigments unmasked. There's a layer of specialist cells at
the join of leaf and stem, the abscission layer, and that's where
the leaves break off, sealing the tree's fluid transport system.

All the trees are accelerating towards the autumnal equinox,
when the clocks change, but we don't. Much.

Change is what happens, the only constant, and although we may
maintain an emotional attachment to an idea of permanence, of our
place in the cosmos being fixed and immutable, that's an illusion.
We are born, we live, and we die. And even then we change. Every
atom of every cell and tissue in our bodies will be recycled.

'What will survive of us is love,' Larkin said, but that's only true if
we're memorialised; in carved images in churches, in words in
a Shakespeare folio, in buildings we've created, or in the children
we have made together.

And they too will change.

> fall is speeding up
> the leaves stop making sugar
> show their true colours

Nightfall

The last light has faded from the sky, the unseen heron has uttered
its goodnight shriek, the jackdaws have stopped chuckling, and
it's time to pull the heavy curtains over the windows. It's not
too cold tonight, so the shutters don't need to be closed.

From the kitchen below, the smells of cooking are wafting up. I
know that supper will be a substantial main course, followed by a
delicious pudding. At home we'd normally only have one course
for supper, or maybe soup for a starter, but I've already had my
soup today at lunch-time. I'm being careful not to over-eat. Losing
weight wasn't easy, and I don't want to have to do it all over again.

After supper it's time for a short practise session with the
saxophone. I use the small library across the courtyard for
this, so that I don't disturb my fellow authors, but the room
is unheated, and the nights have been frosty lately, so I don't
linger. I play just long enough to keep my embouchure in
shape, so that I can resume properly when I get home.

I brought my Japanese book with me—I'm learning to write
hiragana—but I confess the urge to write haibun has overcome
the desire to improve my Japanese.

Then I head for the lounge, to talk with my new friends; I so much
enjoy their company. Some nights we'll play Bananagrams. With
people who love words and language, as we all do, it's a great game
to play. I've learned some new words, and taught them a few useful
ones. Lava flows in two forms, ropey and blocky, and geologists use
the Hawaiian words *pahoehoe* and *aa* to describe them. The latter is
a godsend for this game, and we've had a lot of laughs along the way.

After supper I'll go back to my room and do some more writing
before I turn in. And in the morning I'll be awake early and eager
to start writing before breakfast. The words and ideas have flowed,
easily and non-stop, the whole time I've been here. It's been intense,

but I haven't felt under pressure. I look back on my Hawthornden Fellowship as one of the best experiences of my writing life, and I think every writer should try living in a castle. At least once.

> shutting out the night
> winter cold approaches soon
> warmth of hearth and friends

Section II

Into the mountains

Bullet train to Nagoya, then a 'limited express' to Takayama. This takes us through the mountains, amid Japanese autumn scenery at its most poetic. The trees are a russet and green mosaic of broadleaves and conifers. Fall is complete on the highest tops, the forest dissolving into transparency, the soft fuzzy look of bare twigs on the high ridges. Downslope the occasional blaze of a scarlet maple or the piercing yellow of a ginkgo tree. The single-track line crosses and re-crosses narrow gorges, with fast green rivers far below. We pass through a metamorphic belt of schists and quartzites and into granite country, the high hard core of Japan.

Takayama is a nice little town of gridded streets, with the Miya River running through it. It has a colourful market and several traditional (without chairs) restaurants, a sake brewery and a miso manufacturer, where we see huge barrels of fermenting bean paste, the very dark 'hatcho' variety. Back home I often make miso soup for my lunch, with bean paste, a few noodles, some vegetables and a sprinkling of dashi powder made from dried bonito flakes.

During the Shogunate period the local administrator lived in a house now restored. The large, high-ceilinged, unheated rooms must have been freezing in winter, even with the open hearths and cooking firepits in the centres of rooms. But sliding back the paper panelling, we see the courtyard garden is full of autumn colour and elegant plants.

> rivers cutting deep
> into ancient granite rocks
> Japan's hard pink heart

Autumn tints

It's good to be here at this time of year. Each day the light is different, as more and more leaves fall from the trees, thinning the cover. The colours in the remaining trees change too, some becoming paler, others darker.

A sudden gust of wind sends lighter leaves fluttering as they fall—that'll be the birches then—while the heavier leaves of sycamore fall more quickly, more directly. Updraughts send leaves aloft like drifts of butterflies, before their inevitable descent.

Yesterday I saw a buzzard try to catch a pigeon, the flash of white below its broad wings as it dived and ducked to avoid the treetops. But it was too slow, and easily outmanoeuvred. Today another buzzard—or it may have been the same one—circled in the glen, slowly gaining height.

The fungi are prolific too; I came across a puffball today, with an open pore. I tapped it with my stick, and the spores puffed out like brown smoke. I also found a troop of bright petrol-blue fungi, their colour suggesting it may not be advisable to try them. At the side of the path, there are many more agarics in different sizes, shapes, colours and states of decay. There's a big brown fungus on a dead tree trunk by the path, no doubt the cause of its downfall. Underfoot there's a carpet of fallen acorns and dropped yew and rowan berries. It's always struck me as strange that birds won't pick up fallen fruit; most will only eat it if it is picked fresh from the branch. In former times wild boar, the scavengers of the forest floor, would have had a feast on these leavings.

It's lovely now, but looking at what's growing here now, and what's passed, spring must be equally beautiful, if not more so, and summer a leafy paradise. And the winter to come, with the leaves gone from the broadleaves, and only the yews and other conifers showing green, must look magnificent too, the starkness of the rocky cliff, the rushing river far below, the warm stones of the old castle, the dreams of all who've stayed here.

   pigeons fly too fast
   to be caught by the buzzard
   a shower of leaves

Up in Skye

Not long after we start 'going out together' as they said back in 1963, we decide we'd like to go on a climbing course together in Skye. We join the Scottish Youth Hostel Association and set off by rail, changing at Fort William for the spectacular West Coast route to Mallaig, and the Skye ferry. Then we catch the bus from Armadale to Sligachan, and meet up with our transport to the hostel in Glenbrittle. Our first day is spent training, learning to tie knots, make belays, and climbing the 'practice boulder', which is the size of a house.

Next day we begin the long slog over the bog to the foot of the hills. The walk is horrible; two miles of tracked and rutted squelching black peat, knee-jarring tussocks, and deceptive pools of black water merging into ditches. Even on the drier stretches the peat sticks to boots and leggings, increasing the weight which has to be lifted with each foot, and draining the energy before the climb itself can begin. But there is no alternative way. So many climbers have trodden the routes to the classic climbs that there is no escape from their deep tracks.

After an hour we are in the lower part of Coire Lagan, between two ridges enclosing a cup-shaped inner corrie with its little lochan, and a waterfall spilling over the edge into the lower corrie. We are hugely impressed. The Cuillin Hills are the remains of a central volcanic complex, part of the chain of Tertiary volcanoes which erupted as the Atlantic Ocean floor stretched and thinned. Over a period of several million years there were several volcanic centres on Skye, with lavas, ash deposits, fissure eruptions, cone sheets and ring dykes, all the varied architectures created in such centres. The rocks too are varied, from the smooth, jointed basalt dykes to the coarse rough gabbro from deep within the magma chamber. From a distance they are extremely scenic; close up they are stunning.

Dave, our climbing guide, takes us out to the right-hand wall of the corrie, a seemingly sheer cliff called the Sron na Ciche, and we see an enormous smooth inclined slab of rock, with an overhanging spike sticking out at the top, about half-way along.

'That's the Cioch,' he says, 'That's what we're going to climb.'

> a bulge of cold rock
> at the top of a wet cliff
> graded Difficult

I feel a rush of fear—I'm not really going to climb out on that thing, am I? I've never done this before.

The first part is an enjoyable scramble, zigzagging higher and higher, and the effort makes my heart work harder. I feel exhilarated, and my fear disappears while I am moving. Then we arrive at the foot of the slab we saw from far below. It is a featureless sheet of rough gabbro, set at an angle that looks to vary between 45 and 60°. The jutting bulge of the Cioch, or pap, starts about three-quarters of the way up.

'This is where we rope up,' says Dave. He attaches one end of the rope to his waistband, and the other to you. Then he just steps out and walks up the slab. Just below the Cioch, the underside of the breast, he stops at a little ledge, makes a secure belay, and takes in the slack until the rope is tight between you.

'Climb when ready' he calls down, and you set off. When you reach him, he unties your rope and throws the end down to me. I think, if I'm to be honest, that I'll never be ready to do this, but, as I've been taught, I tie myself on (a bowline and a bight), call out 'Climbing,' and step out. My feet are secure, I can clearly see Dave above me, taking in the rope, but about halfway up I look down and realise I am walking above a one thousand foot precipice. I feel my testicles retract with the fear of it. Instinctively I put my hands on the slab and pull my body in. Dave shouts down that this will put me off balance. He urges me to stand up straight and walk to him. I do as I am told, and soon find myself able to look ahead and upwards, although looking down still gives me the weirdest feeling. I can see the lighter pathway worn in the rock beneath my feet, where countless other climbers have walked before. I make it to the belay.

> from the mountain's snout
> look down on a wee lochan
> regain composure

The next pitch is easier, sticking to the angle between the slab and the massively overhanging Cioch. When my turn comes this time I step out more boldly than I feel, but my confidence grows, and I move surely and rapidly up the good rough rock until we are all on the ledge.

'Now for the Cioch itself' Dave says. 'It's actually a fairly short pitch, you just keep your feet on this ledge here, and hold onto the other ledge above your head, and walk along. There's lots of holds. I'll be directly above you all the time—it's very safe.'

He sets off and we can see him climbing easily up a crack which, in truth, I'd have called a wonky staircase if it had been just a bit lower down. I ease myself out on the ledge. There is nothing below me but air—I am dangling above an abyss. I can see climbers below me setting out on the climb we've just done. They look very small. Forcing myself on, I follow where Dave has led, and come to the crack I'd thought looked easy from below. It doesn't any longer, but I scramble up it and soon find myself on the platform beside him, at the top of the Cioch. It is harder for you, because you are shorter, and it's difficult to stretch up to the crack above, but we both succeed. We stand for a while, sweat cooling. I can't bring myself to go too close to the edge.

The first part of the descent is the reverse of the ascent, but at the top of the slab Dave takes us higher up the ledge, to a point which leads to the summit of the Sgurr Sgumain Ridge, and a track which leads back down to civilisation.

And so the week continues, in fear and excitement, climbing summit after summit. At the end of it we hitchhike to Glencoe, and after a night in the hostel, we head home, by then closer than ever. We have learned to tie knots.

On top of the world

Arriving at the Brahmaputra Grand Hotel in Lhasa we are greeted by
a young man in Tibetan costume standing on the staircase, playing
a long-necked stringed instrument, the *dramyin*, and by a young
woman, beautifully costumed, who sings a song for us from the
opposite staircase. White silk scarves are draped round our necks, a
sign of welcome and blessing, but the guide takes the gloss off it by
saying these *khata* are not the best quality! The hotel doubles as a
museum, but in this museum you can actually buy the artefacts if you
are rich enough. It's just along the road from the military academy,
and the hotel gates are guarded by men in military uniform, although
they seem friendly enough. Then on to the Jokhang Monastery in
Barkhor Square, the central square of the old part of the city, and
the religious heart of Tibet. This is hugely impressive, with very fine
views from its roof. Inside is a beautiful statue of Chenresig, the
boddhisatva of compassion. Pilgrims make a clockwise circle, the
kora, round the old town, the more devout performing the ritual
by prostration. I recall the slanting light coming into the lamasery,
lighting up the faces of two monks in earnest conversation and a
cat dozing nearby. I am puzzled by the fact that most Tibetans keep
their right arms outside their robes, jackets or whatever. I ask about
it, but I get the singularly unhelpful reply that, 'It's just a custom.'

> where are your armies?
> outside my sleevies

Then to Sera, a complex of temples. one of the most prominent
monasteries in Tibet. Buddhists were most brutally treated during
and after the Chinese invasion (I refuse to call it a 'liberation', as
do the Chinese) of 1950, and then the religion was suppressed in
the Cultural Revolution. In recent years, its potential for attracting
tourists has been recognised, and the authorities are less strict,
although riots and disturbances still occur. Mandalas are spiritual
maps, organised around square and circular patterns, highly
embellished and decorated. At Sera, as in other monasteries, they
are made of coloured sand, intricately poured by groups of monks

with very steady hands. Usually they are destroyed on completion—the act of making them is itself the important religious act. But here at Sera a fine example is kept on permanent display. I do not understand its meaning, but I can admire the skill of those who made it. In another building, the Scripture Printing Room, prayer scrolls are individually printed by hand, then assembled into books or placed inside *mani*, prayer wheels. The debating courtyard is deservedly famous. Each day groups of novices assemble, to debate scriptural questions posed by the teaching monks. It is high-spirited and very good natured, punctuated by hands clapping and feet stamping. It has to be said, however, that foot stamping is less emphatic when wearing modern trainers, which are common here.

> ink on the roller
> lean forward to print the sheet
> lean back and repeat

At the Barkhor market, I buy prayer shawls, a scarf, a mani wheel and prayer beads. In the Jokhang temple, the stone pavement in front of the sacred images is regularly wiped with a mixture of water and yak butter, so the pilgrims can slide their wooden hand-blocks more easily over the floor when prostrating. The land used to be ruled by the priesthood, but even the present Dalai Lama has acknowledged that there can be no return to theocracy if the country ever regains autonomy. It's most unlikely now, since more than 50% of the Tibetan population is now ethnic Han Chinese.

Up early on another beautiful morning for a drive to the Potala Palace. We have a strict security check on entry—bags X-rayed etc—then up the first set of steps to a passport check. The walk up the main staircase is exhausting at this altitude (3,700m at the top), and we have to stop frequently to rest. Once at the top, however, the views of the city are magnificent. As a temple, however, I feel it lacks something. I'm not really all that interested in previous Dalai Lamas and their burial monuments, albeit that some of the tombs are bejewelled works of art. There is one big triple Buddha statue (past, present and future Buddhas—Vairocana, Shakyamuni and Maitreya) but the one in the Jokhang is far

more impressive. We walk down the sloping ramp to our coach
for the short drive to Norbulingka and the Summer Palace.

> white palace, blue sky
> prayer flags on long poles, incense
> up on left, down right

A relaxing walk along a tree-lined avenue leads to a beautiful
golden palace in a lovely autumn garden. This palace was built
in 1954 by the present Dalai Lama, before he fled in 1959. Most of
the rooms are fairly austere, except the bathroom, which is 1950s
modern. Bar-headed geese are swimming in the moat or walking
about on the artificial island in the middle. One has a broken wing;
another is making half-hearted attempts to brood an egg, which
must have been addled in the spring. Outside the gate I help one of
our party haggle for a singing bowl. The seller is so pleased to sell
it that I feel we must have been overcharged. Anyway, she gives us
each a free bracelet and a hug. I like the Tibetans I've met here.

> ancient radio
> an old gift from India
> new fitted bathroom
> all 1950s vintage
> and sacred paintings on walls

Our guide promises us a 'Tibetan Cultural Experience' in the
Mad Yak Café (I'm not making it up—that's what it's called) that
evening. I don't much like the barley beer or the salty yak butter
tea, but the 'Sheep & Potatoes' soup is good, as is the steamed
yak meat bun. I don't try the 'Sheep Sausage' (black pudding)
or the 'Sheep Lungs'. It's silly to be squeamish, I know, but there
you go. The yak yoghourt is delicious, but I can't attempt the
yak 'cheesecake'. It smells awful, and I see a yak hair in it.

The entertainment is, frankly, dire. but I hadn't expected
authenticity. Chinese waiters and waitresses don traditional
Tibetan costume and wave their arms around on a small stage,
succeeded by singers who mime badly to a crackly tape, and

most of the songs are in Chinese anyway, not Tibetan. Leaving the place, I say to you, 'Now I have the title for my next book.' And so I had—*The Floorshow at the Mad Yak Café*.

> not quite cabaret—
> not singers, not dancers, but
> a taste of Tibet

I wonder if there's going to be any trace of indigenous Tibetan culture left in 10 years, here or in Qinghai? And yet, seeing the devotion of the Tibetan peasants, I can't help hoping that it will be a long time before they're converted to the Chinese way of life. And I wasn't surprised by the ethnic riot that erupted the following year, just after the Chinese Olympics.

Getting down to it

I don't remember much about getting to the top of Ben Lawers the first time I climbed it, but I remember the agonies of the descent very well. The path seems endless, the constant switch-backs in direction hurt my arthritic knees with each downward step, each jolt of boot on ground, even with a pair of walking poles. Part of the problem is that I can see the car park at the bottom, and it seems an endless distance away. It just never seems to get any closer. As I stumble down I deliberately force myself not to look at the visitor centre, but look instead at the stones and mud beneath my feet, trying to decide on the geological origin of each pebble from the sequence on the mountain—Farragon Group, Loch Tay Limestone, Lawers Schist, Green Beds. The wildflowers beside the track I'd taken such pleasure in on the way up are totally ignored. After each ten minutes or so of mind-numbing pebble-watching, I look down the glen to see if the visitor centre is any bigger, but no, it hasn't taken any miraculous leap nearer. It's a relief to move into a gully away from the line of sight, and for half-an-hour or so my consciousness is all in my staggering feet, and in my agonizingly swollen knees.

By the scattered stones of an abandoned steading, a blue-veined white butterfly rests on a dry grass stalk, waiting to die. Its biological purpose served, there is nothing else for it to do. With us, there is raising, and teaching, telling stories, and still growing before growing still.

> sitting very still
> seeing the distant mountains
> move against the clouds
> golden gorse carpets the slopes,
> scatttered cattle on the skyline

Into the Valley

Leaving Fresno the day after our Yosemite tour we stop at a roadside stall selling fresh fruit grown locally—lunch will be sweet, juicy and delicious. After Bakersfield we come to a huge sprawling windfarm set up on the slopes of the Tehachapi Pass. Never having seen giant wind turbines before, I think of spinning crucifixions in the near constant breeze blowing through the Central Valley. From here it's downhill into the Mojave Desert, and our first sight of its characteristic plants.

I've grown cacti and other succulent plants for many years, became a bit of a specialist, but this is the first time I've seen this xerophytic vegetation in its proper habitat. Joshua trees, cholla cactus, creosote bushes and many other desert plants would dominate our surroundings in the days to come.

Mojave itself has a graveyard for unwanted aircraft—row after row of 707s, Jumbos and many other types all parked in the dry desert air, engines wrapped in plastic for protection. I didn't discover if this is just a dump, or if some planes are cannibalised for spare parts.

Our route took us through Ridgecrest and Trona next, the latter being named for the natron, sodium carbonate, which used to be mined here. Then the road swept round a bend and we had our first view of the Panamint Mountains and Death Valley.

Coming in over the Towne Pass, our guide puts a CD in the player by the bus driver, and I am astonished to recognise Terry Riley's minimalist classic, 'In C'. It is an inspired choice of music for the descent, past arroyos and gravel ridges dotted with big barrel cacti, low-growing Mormon Tea (*Ephedra*) and other desert plants, in the growing heat. The air conditioning system in the bus cannot fully cope with the temperature, but reduces it considerably. We step out of the bus at Furnace Creek, which lives up to its name. The heat strikes our faces with an almost palpable impact. This is the most extreme environment I've encountered

up to this point. I am lost in admiration for the pioneering
settlers who took this uncompromising, and sometimes lethal,
route to the coast. Covered wagons can cover only so much.

> coping desert plants
> ancient aircraft parked
> on shadeless sand

Saved from drowning

Into the Shokawa Valley, the bus driver having to cope with hairpin bends, narrow twisting tunnels, dams, lakes and hydro-electric schemes. In places the scenery is much like the Scottish Highlands, in others very different. By a large lake behind a gravity dam stands a huge cherry tree with spreading branches, bare of leaves at this time of year. Before the valley was submerged a local doctor transplanted the much-loved tree to a place of safety, above the rising waters. For several years the tree showed no sign of life, then it began to put out a few leaves. Now it is flourishing, and there is a statue here to the man who moved it, and quite rightly. I've never seen such a large tree survive a transplanting. Incidentally, 'cherry' in a Japanese poem means the blossom, whereas with us it's the fruit.

The hamlet of Ogimachi is in the Shirakawa-go district (not the Shirakawa Barrier of Basho, which is much further south). This is a World Heritage Site, for its preservation and display of the unique *gassho-zuchuri* houses. Gassho refers to hands raised together in prayer, because the roofs are pitched at sixty degrees to shed snow in the severe winters they experience here. They're also very practical, as the airy roof space is used for silk worm production, while the ground floor is occupied by extended families of 20 or 30 individuals. The roof is thatched with *Miscanthus*, a kind of pampas grass we see growing by the viewpoint above the flat-floored valley.

The descent to Matsumoto is by a road as spectacular as the earlier one, and the driver experiences great difficulties with the sharp bends inside some of the tunnels. We feel for him. The huge wooden castle here was built in 1504 as a home for the *daimyo*, the feudal overlord. It has many defensive features—a moat, steep staircases between floors, and a nightingale floor, whose nails 'sang' if anyone walked on it, giving warning to the guards. In the grounds we are entertained by another chrysanthemum show, and by the long and frankly incomprehensible folkloric Tale of Hare Meat Soup.

> prayer roofs shed snow
> shelter silkworms in valley
> where north wind doth blow

Loch Turret

We used to have a caravan in Comrie, Perthshire, on a site called
Twenty Shilling Wood. The caravan had belonged to my parents,
and they let us have it when my father retired and bought a house in
the village. The site was named for the value of the annual harvest
of oak bark from the coppiced woodland for use in the tanning
industry. It was an ideal place for trips to local beauty spots, and
adventures further afield. Higher up the glen, the Lednock Dam
had been built as part of the post-war Breadalbane Hydro-Electric
Scheme, by labourers billeted in wooden cabins by the roadside.
After the dam and its associated tunnels, stream channels and
turbines were finished, the site was sold on, and a local entrepreneur
demolished the huts and used their concrete bases as hard standings
for caravans. The site is unobtrusive, back from the road and
concealed by birch trees, which also separate the vans, so there
is a degree of privacy you don't normally get in caravan parks.

When the children were young it was a great place to take
them on weekends. We'd drive up on Saturday afternoons, and
as the car rounded a sharp bend and I had my first glimpse
of Ben Halton and Ben Vorlich I felt the tensions of the
working week draining away. Our pleasures were low-key—
walks in the woods or in the hills, barbecues, bird watching,
attempting to keep dry, visits to my parents and the like.

Several times we walked along the track beside Loch Turret, another
part of the Hydro scheme, with every small stream captured and
channelled to feed underground tunnels. I recall one walk in
particular. On the skyline in front of a small vertical crag, two
ravens are engaged in a flying contest—or that's the way it looks.
Probably part of a courtship ritual, we guess. They fly round
each other, spiralling closer and closer, until they almost touch.
Then they break suddenly, one flying almost upside down below
the other—claws outstretched. Sometimes feet lock briefly, and
both birds spin together in a ball of ragged black feathers. The
aerodynamic forces due to their unnatural positions ruffles their

wings and breaks up their normally streamlined profiles. We watch them for maybe ten minutes, enthralled and delighted, before moving off along the path. Below the crag is a scree slope—sharp-angled boulders of pink felsite rock. We hear a 'chack-chack' sound, almost like stones being struck together. Far up the slope we see the blackbird-sized bird which made the noise; the white neck-band identifying it as a ring ouzel, a new tick in my bird book.

Glen Turret, and the track at the far end leading up to Ben Chonzie, is a great place for mountain hares. They didn't seem to have any fear of humans, at least those walking without dogs, and they'd sometimes just squat on the path and look at us. They're beautiful animals, and tough as nails, staying at altitude throughout the winter, when their coats change from brown to white. That was fine in the olden days, when snow in winter was dependable, but our milder winters means the poor beasties, instead of being camouflaged, stand out like surrender flags.

> happy camping days
> in the hills with our two boys
> hiding in the trees

Have some Madeira, m'dear

Our walking guide for the levada walk tries to scare us by warning of the perils of the day ahead; the narrowness of the paths, the steepness of the cliffs below, the slipperiness underfoot, and to pay strict attention to His Commands. We drive to Ribeiro Frio—Cold River—and park outside Victor's Restaurant, buying crisps and Mars bars for the day ahead. It's actually quite cold at the start—the log fire in the restaurant isn't just for show. We set off through a tiny botanical garden planted up with the local endemics—the 'Laurisylva' vegetation (which is very rare anywhere these days). We start on the shadow side of the mountain, and in the shade. We've been issued with walking poles, and I'm glad of mine for extra security on the trickier bits of the descent. It's mostly very easy walking, all downhill, following the little levada channel, either on the path or on top of the concrete or dressed stone channel wall, but there are often precipices on the downslopes, and the exposure can be 'interesting'. The levadas were made to capture rainwater, and to feed it down to reservoirs near the towns. On a small volcanic island with limited rainfall and rapid run-off from the steep slopes, it's an ingenious and practical solution. They criss-cross the island, following the contour lines, and the paths, built for maintenance, have become a tourist attraction for those who enjoy walking.

Soon we encounter clearings where the sun shines, and we get magnificent views of the high peaks across the valley. I'm highly impressed with the laurisylva vegetation—so many mosses and liverworts in particular—far richer than in most Scottish woods. Eventually we leave the levada and follow the steep track down to Portela, a little bar, for a cool drink, and the bus back to base in Funchal. It's been an exhilarating day. In the evening we dine on espada—scabbard fish—because it's the touristy thing to do. Jane has hers with banana, I with exotic fruit. Sounds weird but it works. The tiny Madeiran bananas are the tastiest I've ever eaten.

> bananas with fish?
> a sweet and salty combo
> for an island meal

Next day the West Tour, a long, all-day excursion. Our first stop is in Camara de Lobos, named for the monk seals—wolves of the sea. Crowds of sullen men stand round the fountain or down by the harbour. They smoke, they spit, they glare at tourists. There's a strong smell of urine by the harbour wall. The brightly coloured boats which Winston Churchill painted here in the 1950s hold no charm.

We drive on and park at the spectacular viewpoint of the Cabo de Girão—reputedly the second-highest promontory in Europe. It's not quite as vertical as St John's Head in Orkney but it's nearly as impressive. The amplified pan pipes of the fake Andean folk group don't add to its attraction. All the same, my feeling of vertigo increases alarmingly as I approach the iron railing. I can't look over it. Back in the bus we move on to Ribeiro Brava—the Wild River—which is anything but. Indeed, as it reaches the sea it becomes an open sewer, discharging black smelly water into a suspiciously cloudy sea. Later I'm always wary of stretches of cloudy water with patches of persistent scum. The place has a tunnel through the cliff into the harbour. There's a nice waterfall tumbling down to the sea, and the cliffs are very picturesque.

From here we drive to a point overlooking Ponta do Sol—the sunniest spot on Madeira. This is our jumping-off point for the sojourn into the mountains. We reach a high grassy plateau—the only place on the island where cows can graze freely. It reminds us both of parts of Scotland. Then a descent down a hair-pin road to Porto Moniz—an attractive little village with natural bathing pools in the volcanic rocks (fresh-looking lava here), dammed with concrete rims to retain the seawater. A view to the east reveals a rock stack with a double window in it—at least that's what it looks like—a huge '8'. I'm impressed by the many plants of *Aeonium tabuliforme* growing out of the vertical cliffs. The road then skirts the coast, sometimes passing through tunnels, past a series of spectacular waterfalls, before rising very steeply to a high point—the watershed of Boca de Encumeada—where we can see both sides of the island. A rapid descent down a series of hairpins to the Pousada de Vinhaticos—another fine viewpoint, then down to the motorway and return to Funchal.

tours of Madeira
fine volcanic scenery
set in the ocean

On Friday we set off for the 'Nun's Valley'—Curral de Freiras to
give it its Sunday name. Perhaps the most spectacular mountain
scenery of the whole trip. Here nuns (and others) sought safety from
marauding pirates, in a high valley very difficult to reach before the
road was built. But first we go back to Camara de Lobos, where we do
the untouristy thing of avoiding the main street and walking round to
the harbour by the poor quarter. I've never seen such poverty. Hovels
with dirt floors, a boy staring into the interior of a 'room' through a
broken plank which was the door, a little beggar girl who follows us
down to the harbour, everyone cowed and resentful. I understand
now the looks of the fishermen. These people can see no future.

Anyway, up in the mountains we climb to a viewpoint—the
Eira do Serra—before descending to the little village for a
piece of genuine Madeira cake and a glass of freshly prepared
poncha, made with *aguardente* (a very rough cane spirit),
honey and lemon juice. I like it. Back down to Funchal, pursued
and overtaken on a hairpin by a group of boy cyclists.

off Africa's coast
botanical paradise
going bananas

The Philosopher's Walk

In a warm sunny autumn day we set off on the excellent Kyoto bus service to the stop closest to the Philosopher's Walk. The Walk follows an aqueduct lined with cherry trees, now bare, along the base of the Eastern Mountains. It was given its name because a local philosophy professor, Nishida Kitaro, used to take his daily constitutional walk along its length. Apart from its intrinsic beauty, it's notable for the number and variety of temples and gardens along its route.

Outside the Silver Temple, Ginkaku-ji, we refresh ourselves with green tea ice cream before entering the temple garden. This place fair takes my breath away, as we say in Scotland. A raked gravel Sea of Silver Sand sits next to a truncated cone of sand, the *kogetsudai*, or Moon-Viewing Height. This is a Zen koan in itself, a physical riddle; a viewing platform which can't be used without destroying it! And the whole thing overlooked by an artfully trained Black Pine. Beside a Buddha statue sprinkled by a waterfall, and a pool surfaced by floating autumn leaves, I bow and pay my respects.

Our next temple is Honen-in, a Jodo Zen temple with raked sand gardens—a quiet little gem for silent contemplation. Each plot is raked in a different pattern—wavy, zigzag, crescentic or linear. A single red flower petal floats in the stone trough used for washing hands. Did it fall in there by accident, or was it placed there for aesthetic reasons? I do not know—another riddle.

We have an o-bento lunch in the courtyard of the Otoya-jinja Shinto shrine before moving on to the Eikan-do temple, a complex of linked buildings hosting an art exhibition. We shuffle barefoot from room to room admiring paintings, decorated fabrics, sculptures and ceramics, before visiting the curious Amida Buddha sculpture. It is vaguely hermaphroditic, and the head is turned to one side in a suggestive 'come hither' look. It's unlike any of the other Amida figures I've seen.

> mapping inner worlds
> in riddles, gravel gardens
> and philosophy

Assynt lochan

The walk is a short one, by the standards of ways I've walked
before. The path is sometimes a flat stretch of bare earth
and gravel, sometimes carefully placed flat boulders in
muddy hollows, and sometimes harder stretches on steep
bedrock—the Lewisian gneiss. Scratches carved by the last
glaciers to pass this way are evident, mapping the direction of
ice flow. Not strictly needed here; it's obvious the ice moved
downhill and west to the sea. Where else would it go?

> after rain
> a shower of midges
> clouds that bite

On the loch, beside a patch of white flowered waterlilies, a
black-throated diver is teaching two of its chicks to fish. These
birds keep very low in the water, their centres of gravity in
that element rather than in air. They fly well enough though,
and have to, to repel predators and rivals; small streamlined
heads, dagger beaks outstretched, wings rapidly beating.

The waterlily leaves curl over on the loch's surface, tumbled by a
quick breeze. As they rise and roll I imagine I see again the head
of yesterday's otter giving me the once over. It isn't; that sleek
squirm of fur and intensity has left the loch to the divers, and to
the oars of the fishermen, thrashing their boat into a rising wind.

> alarmed gull
> circles the loch
> crying, crying

Another 'One of the Many Days'

I rise at six, breakfast, and arrive at the Bridge of Orchy car park
before eight, in a heavy shower of rain, which soon passes. I walk up
the road to the station, entered by an underpass below the rail line
leading to the West Highland Way and the path to Beinn Dorain.

Alec Finlay has identified this entrance as the cognate of
Basho's Shitomae Gate. Basho's hokku at his point mentions a
horse and biting fleas. A train arrives and stops at the station,
just above my head. So now I have my opening verse:

> starting gate with
> iron horse overhead
> and new midge bites

I do not expect to encounter bandits on this journey, so I
see no need to employ 'a strong young man' to lead the way
and to act as bodyguard. Besides, I have my walking poles,
and these will serve to ward off any unruly elements.

The meadow is a mass of yellow spikes, each tipped with bright yellow
starry flowers. This is bog asphodel (*Narthecium ossifragum*), one of
my favourite Highland plants. Bell heather (*Erica carnea*) is also in
flower, and profusely. The path rises steadily toward the mountain.

Seen from the main road Beinn Dorain appears as a perfect
cone—a green Fuji-san. However, from the climber's point of
view it's a broad ridge, a double mountain mass, with Beinn an
Dothaidh on the left, and Beinn Dorain on the right, linked by a
col, or bealach. Vertical cliffs on both sides frame the path up the
wall. The route rises steadily, and I notice how badly eroded the
path has become. In places it's more like a wet scree slope, with
loose and unstable gravel. This would trouble me on the descent,
and going up it was, in places, like walking up a stream bed.

> waterfalls left and right

the way up shows no sign
of getting shorter

Views of the surrounding hills become better and better. A gully
on a mountain opposite shows as a white streak of tumbling
water, which at first I mistake for a quartz vein shining in the
sun. An hour into the walk I stop briefly for a cup of tea, and the
midges immediately start biting. They obviously haven't read
the instruction label on my midge repellent spray. The tea—a
wonderful 'Iron Buddha' oolong—refreshes immediately.

monkey picked tea
lifts the climber
up Beinn Dorain

The Beinn Dorain frogs described by Norman MacCaig in 'One
of the Many Days' are numerous and very colourful—green,
yellow, russet, brown. They're active too, hopping or clambering
through the wet grass by the path. I don't know if they're 'tinily
considering / the huge concept of Ben Dorain', but I am.

coloured frogs
leap in the wet grass
as high as Beinn Dorain

The last stretch up to the bealach is quite steep, and then I emerge
onto the broad saddle, marked by a cairn. From here the views
of distant Glen Lyon and its loch are spectacular, and the hills
on both sides are glorious. I see the path leading to Beinn an
Dothaidh, but I take the right-hand fork. I'm soon walking up
boiler-plate slabs of very good rock, up the next steep stretch. A
family of ravens flies overhead, checking out this intruder. I'm the
only human in the landscape—no climbers above or below me.

a brown thread
stitches the walk
to Glen Lyon

        coal black birds
        fly from crag to crag
        croaking

I like walking alone in the hills. It gives me the freedom to make my own pace, much slower than when I was young, and I can notice little things as I walk. At this height—over 3000ft by now—I see the first signs of Scotland's Arctic-Alpine flora. Alpine Lady's Mantle (*Alchemilla alpina*) is common, with leaves like small green hands, and topped by clusters of greenish flowers. I also see Starry Saxifrage (*Saxifraga stellaris*), and, more rarely, a true mountain flower, *Sibbaldia procumbens*, which has no common name. Small and delicate, this flower is the botanical emblem of the Royal Botanic Garden Edinburgh, the place where I worked for fourteen years. It is named for Sir Robert Sibbald, a co-founder of the Garden in 1670, whose book *Scotia Illustrata* first described some of Scotland's distinctive plants, animals, birds and fishes. It's not just for the pace that I like climbing alone, however; it's for the peace. Only I am here, with my senses and my thoughts, no distractions.

        asphodel
        bell heather
        saxifrage

There are sheep on a grassy meadow just below the summit ridge. They graze in pairs, ewe and lamb, and if the lamb should stray too far, the mother bleats until her adventurous daughter comes back. It's hard not to feel sorry for sheep, out in all weathers, driven high in summer, driven low in winter to have the fat lambs taken for the table. But it's also hard to feel sorry for sheep, seeing the amount of habitat change they have caused, eating all tree shoots that emerge from hidden seeds, so that only grasses, sedges, woodrush and small herbs cover the ground. And the Clearances too were caused by human greed for the income the sheep could provide.

        high in the hills
        with old poets
        in my head

The steep sections of climb are beginning to catch up with my aging body. I get severe cramps in my upper thigh muscles, which force me to sit on boulders and massage my legs until the pain eases. I've never had this before, and I reflect that I really should climb more often, so that my muscles and tendons will be strengthened.

Just below the final ridge I look up and see, silhouetted against the skyline, a mountain hare, the two long ears raised. He turns to look at me, unafraid. His only enemy at this great height would be a golden eagle, but I have not seen one today. Nor have I seen any deer, so I cannot reflect on Duncan Ban MacIntyre's epic Gaelic poem 'Beinn Dorain', which I have read in a fine translation by Iain Crichton Smith. What I do see now, and it's a lovely sight too, are small clumps of Purple Saxifrage (*Saxifraga oppositifolia*), a gorgeous wee flower.

> hare on the hill
> long ears swivel—
> wind sounds

I climb out onto the summit plateau, pass the cairn and walk on to reach the true summit. The view from here is worthy of the climb. A large part of Scotland's mountain landscape is laid out before me—Ben Nevis to the north-west, Cruachan to the west, the Lawers group and the rest of the Breadalbane Hills to the east, and south to the Crianlarich group, most of which I've climbed in years past. I can see thick dark grey mists in some distant glens, signs of rainstorms. I stop here, back to the wind, for my lunch, and more tea from my flask, before beginning the long walk back.

> grey smirr of rain
> in distant glen—
> someone's getting wet

The descent is fine as far as the bealach, but after that it becomes tricky because of the loose gravel in the path. It's at the bealach that I have my first human encounter of the day, with a family of foreign tourists who ignore my greeting. I slip and slide, overbalance when stones tip and wobble, and jar my knees when I take an over-long step. Feet and ankles are painful too, with the constant twisting and flexing. At times I curse myself, feeling that I've taken on too much at my age. But slowly and inexorably the Bridge of Orchy houses get nearer.

> a foot placed
> on shoogly stones
> twists an ankle

At the end of the walk I drive back to Comrie through a torrential downpour until I reach my mother's house. Time for a glass of Japanese malt whisky (courtesy of Alec), a hot bath, a meal, and bed. The mountain is left to the frogs, the ravens, the hare, the flowers, and to poetry.

Viva, Las Vegas

Leaving Death Valley Junction behind, we stop at the viewpoint at the head of the pass to look back at the spectacular scenery. We have a fine view of Zabriskie Point, famous for the film of the same name, and I take a photo of it which now hangs in my study beside the one of Yosemite. It was named for a Polish-born engineer who worked in one of the many mines in the Valley. Borax, soda, and other minerals were worked here, the result of the evaporation of a vast inland sea which once filled the valley. Clouds are building, and the forecast is for a storm, a very infrequent occurrence here. While the rain itself will be welcome, it usually falls so abruptly and so heavily that it causes flash floods. It's always been the way things happen here, and the plants and animals have adapted to it.

Over the border into Nevada now, and a curious town called Pahrump, where brothels are legal and heavily advertised, but we bus passengers are not tempted to sample the delights of the many 'erotic menus' on offer. Then we are taken deeper into the desert, driving through an area where gypsum had been mined, or maybe was still being mined. Behind the padlocked wire fences of the concessions, we can see the heaps of white powder which cover the landscape. Within sight of the distant Red Rock Canyon massif, which looks rather majestic, we have a rest stop at a gas station. While the others stretch their legs or use the rest rooms, I potter about among the vegetation, trying to recognise as many plants as I can—barrel cacti, paperflowers, mesquite, yuccas, chollas and other desert specialists—while keeping my eyes open for any snakes which may be taking a siesta in their shade.

Then it's down the road to Las Vegas. We hit The Strip and park at Luxor for lunch. We walk through its enormous atrium awestruck and open-mouthed. Our own hotel is Circus! Circus! (you need the exclamation marks). Our driver and guide cannot believe that we could come to Las Vegas and not gamble, but them's the facts—we don't gamble, unless you count Premium Bonds. In the evening, after a meal in the hotel's vast casino, we meet up for a walking tour of the other hotels. The Bellagio has a spectacular show of dancing fountains, choreographed to Frank Sinatra songs; Caesar's Palace has a Roman-themed design, and we see a pirate attack and a volcanic eruption beside other hotels whose names I have forgotten. Finally, to the Fremont Street Experience, where thousands of coloured LEDs are suspended above the street where the Golden Nugget casino's croupiers are on strike. At 8pm the lights go on, to show an animated cartoon version of a quick history of the world, from the birth of the Solar System. Can you use the word gobsmacked in a haibun? I think I have to.

The thing about Vegas is that its over the top man-made features are of a piece with the natural wonders of the Southwest. You just *have* to go there.

> pale desert mountains
> desolate, jagged, remote
> life taking chances

Back to North Uist

Driving through Kintail I see a black hill where no black hill should be. Burnt tree stumps are evidence of a great fire here, and not very long ago. The whole hillside is scorched and blackened from shore to summit. In gullies there are a few green trees, but here too their lower limbs have been burned. The road circles round Loch Duich, and all the way round the same funereal trees. There are several houses by the roadside, but none appear to have been damaged.

We stop overnight at Kyle of Lochalsh, and in the morning head over the Skye bridge and on to Uig for the ferry to Lochmaddy. The short crossing is uneventful until I see a whale. A black arc with a proportionally small fin arches out of the water momentarily and is gone. No flukes break the surface, so my guess is Minke. I'm so shocked and excited that I can't say anything, and by the time I stammer, 'I've just seen a whale,' it has sounded, and none of the other passengers see it.

We arrive in Kirkibost in warm sunshine, just as a pair of greylag geese land in the field next door. We find our cottage—Grand View (and it has)—and as advertised the key is under a stone by the front door. Stepping out of the back gate into the field of rough grass we see a group of red deer hinds. From a fenced-off exclosure we hear a corncrake. A wheatear, not long arrived from its African holiday, perches on the stone wall. A snipe flies over, performing its display flight, with the well-known drumming noise. After our evening meal however, the sky is blotted out by driving rain, and a flash of lightning lights up the low clouds.

Next day we drive north and catch our first glimpse, 40 miles offshore, of the St Kilda archipelago, the rocky islands of Dun, Hirta, Boreray, Soay and Stac an Armin. The view is so clear that we can see white water at the base of the cliffs.

> burnings and birds
> a Minke in the Minch
> these stormy islands

Some steps on the Southern Upland Way

From the War Memorial in Cockburnspath I walk along the path
by a field's edge. I recall how this was home, in the early 1880s, to
a group of artists who called themselves 'The Boys', now better
known as 'The Glasgow Boys'. James Guthrie's masterwork—*A
Hind's Daughter*—was painted here, as were others by Henry,
Melville, Walton, Crawhall and others. The Boys were the
subject of a wonderful exhibition in the Kelvingrove Museum in
Glasgow. Muriel Gray made a TV programme about them, and
members of the Dunbar Art Club posed in Co'path and at Cove
Harbour to lend a bit of 'modren' authenticity to the film.

> girl in the painting
> silvery knife held down
> a threat to cabbages

The path turns sharply here and follows an underpass below the A1
and the East Coast Main Line, before crossing a minor road at Cove
Farm and heading down to Cove village. It's a common enough name
in Scotland, Cove, but this is one I've been visiting since I was a wee
boy in the 1950s. The field edge here is splotched with the bright
spikes of marsh orchids, and from the hedges and fields the sounds of
Grasshopper Warblers, Meadow Pipits, Willow Warblers and Skylarks
fill the air. There's a warm scent of Sweet Cicely in the air too, and the
ground herbs include Dove's Foot Cranesbill, buttercups, campions
and coltsfoot.

> yellowhammer
> in the gorse bush—
> good camouflage

At the path's junction above the Cove clifftop I make a detour
to the hamlet, to see a new bronze sculpture commemorating
the loss of 11 out of 21 Cove fishermen in the East Coast fishing
disaster of 1881, along with many others from fishing towns
along the coast, with Eyemouth bearing the highest death toll.

some drowned
within sight of families—
the price of fish

The path carries on, with several new jinks and stiles to avoid
landslips. This coast is eroding very rapidly, the red clay capping the
vertically-dipping rocks being sloughed off all along the route, leaving
the green slopes punctuated by red scars. Efforts at stabilisation
now focus on planting trees—willow, holly, hawthorn, briar and the
occasional rowan. Their intertwined roots offer the best chance of
holding back the soil, but for how long?

deep roots of horsetails
holding on
for dear life

The path now reaches the cliff overlooking the beautiful Pease Bay. I
see the big waves rolling in to break on the sandy shore, and wonder
why there are no surfers here today. The next steps will take me up
Pease Dean, and into Penmanshiel Woods, but that's for another day.
I listen to watersounds on the bridge over the Cockburnspath Burn,
a bubbling rill on one side of the path, and a waterfall on the other.

an orange
quenches the thirst
sufficiently

Nijubashi

In the Ginza district we walk through an underground arcade,
calling in at a pearl wholesaler's shop. The cultured pearl industry
was big in Japan, at the height of the popularity of pearl jewellery.
It was started by the Nishikawa and Mikimoto families, although
based on a discovery by the British biologist William Savile-
Kent. Staff are trained to insert small pieces of shell into the
mantle of the living mollusc. A proportion of them begin the
process of accreting layers of aragonite round the foreign body
to form pearls. At maturity the oysters are harvested, opened
and inspected. The pearls are graded by roundness, colour and
size, before ending up in shops like this one in the Ginza and
being traded on world-wide to make necklaces and jewellery. The
oyster meat goes for food production, raw, cooked or smoked,
and the shells are ground up for recycling. Nothing is wasted.

As for ourselves, we do not feel any desire to buy pearls,
but next door we find a *tonkatsu* restaurant and dine on its
speciality—breaded pork chops served on shredded cabbage
with a tangy sauce closely resembling our familiar HP brand.

We walk through Hibiya Park and see the first down-and-outs we've
encountered in Japan. Being unemployed here is a matter of shame,
a thing to be hidden. These people hide themselves away from their
fellow city dwellers, sleep under blue plastic sheets. Unlike in the
main streets of Western cities, we do not see beggars. Here they live
a shadow existence beside the feral cats patrolling the park. The
cats are keenly interested in groups of Asian crows, which have a
distinctive call. And the crows keep their wary eyes on the cats.

This being November there is, naturally, a chrysanthemum show
in the Park. It's the national flower of Japan, here displayed in an
astonishing variety of colours, varieties and floral arrangements.

Approaching the Imperial Palace grounds the avenues are
lined with statuesque Japanese Black Pine (*Pinus thunbergii*),

much admired by the locals, and impeccably trained for display. In the fading light we reach the Nijubashi Bridge and watch carp and turtles in the Imperial waters.

> stiff egret fishes
> just one leg in the water
> the bridge stands on two

The Hebridean wave

The Calmac ferry noses past the skerries, which seem alarmingly close to the hull, and performs its reverse pirouette in the harbour, coming to a halt by the jetty in Lochboisdale.

I drive off with my passengers—two humans and a dog, At the end of the village the road becomes single track with passing places, like the Highland roads I remember so well from my childhood. I like to think I'm a polite driver, giving consideration to my fellow road users. I was to discover that most drivers in the Uists are equally polite, if not more so.

At first, pulling into passing places, or passing cars which had similarly pulled in, I give the cheery full-hand open-palm signal I would use in Dunbar High Street, thanking drivers for letting me pull out behind the double-parked Co-op truck. I quickly came to understand that this would be regarded here as unnecessarily extrovert, verging on the flamboyant.

The Hebridean signal, which I quickly adopt, is the raising of the left forefinger from the steering wheel, by an amount not greater than an inch, for any higher than an inch would be showy and wasteful of energy. The roads are quiet by southern standards, but busy enough. On most roads I encounter oncoming cars, motor caravans and other vehicles, and we always acknowledge each other, the raised finger taking the place of the salute or the doffed cap of earlier times. Cyclists are always given extra consideration, a tribute to their heroic efforts pushing against strong headwinds and driving rain. Sheep are an unpredictable hazard, and a flock of greylag geese taking off and flying across the road at windscreen height is a bonus.

Causeways on the Uists link the low-lying islands; the major ones of South Uist, Benbecula, Grimsay and North Uist, and the smaller ones, including the one leading to our cottage on Baleshare. I also loved the bilingual road signs, trying to work out the equivalence in pronunciation of the English and Gaelic names. Loch nam Madath, Circheboist, and Bearnaraigh.

Journeys here are never non-stop; they're punctuated by
necessary halts, places to give way, to make allowances,
to demonstrate empathy. These are the most civilised and
civilising roads in Scotland, and long may they remain so.

> the narrow roads
> of the Western Isles
> lower blood pressure

"I'm on the train"

Having waited in the Distinguished Guests Lounge at Xining station, Qinghai Province (though we didn't feel particularly distinguished), we board the Qingzang high-altitude train around midnight. There are four of us in our sleeping car; Jane and I, plus two women friends from our party, and we quickly settle in to our bunks to sleep.

By seven the next morning we are in Golmud, a halt of about half an hour, and the sky is beginning to lighten. The toilet doors are kept locked in the station, so we are all a bit cross-legged and desperate by the time the train pulls out, now reinforced by a fresh complement of Peoples Liberation Army officers, wearing caps too big for their heads. Our sleeping car converts to a day cabin with large windows, and the corridor opposite also has large viewing windows. The first mountain range crossed by the train is the Kunlun Shan, a series of west-east trending mountains on the northern side of the Tibetan Plateau. The summits in the Burhan Budai Shan and Bayar Hor Shan are snow-covered, and we can see frozen ground below us. The track is raised above the permafrost on huge concrete pillars—an amazing feat of engineering. As the train swings round long bends we can see the massive locos at either end pulling and pushing us along. Crossing bridges, we look down on frozen rivers, although there is little snow at this altitude. The ground is mostly bare and ochre coloured.

It isn't until we leave the mountains and move into the Tanggula Shan steppe that we start to see vegetation, and the animals that depend on it. The grasses and forbs form a glaucous-green carpet in this section of Tibet, or Xizang Zizhiqi Autonomous Territory, as the authorities name it.

The kiang, a native wild ass, is the dominant grazer here. They seem quite plentiful, and unafraid of the train, coming quite close to us. Their coats are a warm chocolate brown, with lighter coloured legs and abdomens, and quite stockily built. We also see a lot of Tibetan gazelle, pale buff, the males sporting horns, the females without.

I'd hoped to see chiru, the Tibetan antelope, but they are elusive.

Birds of prey are common—lammergeyer, golden eagle, red
kite and ravens. We also catch rare glimpses of pika, a rodent-
like relative of the rabbit, and one sight of its main predator,
the Tibetan sand fox, a most peculiar square-jawed fox with
short stumpy legs. And by the side of a river, I'd guess a
tributary of the Brahmaputra, a magnificent wild bull yak.

Our high point is 5,076m, 16,533 feet above sea level—higher
than the summit of Mont Blanc. My sinuses are painful and
bleeding from the altitude, but otherwise I am fine. We come
alongside Lake Namtso, turquoise, but muddy brown and slushy
near the shore, where it is starting to freeze with the approach
of winter. Flocks of bar-headed geese, numerous ducks, and
a species of gull with red legs, paddle in the shallows.

With the train running late, the descent from Amdo to Lhasa
seems to take ages. We are passing settlements now, small farms
with mud-brick walls, and dust devils raised by the motor bikes
of the yak herders. We arrive at Lhasa station to find no luggage
trolleys, and a long trek to the bus park, but we have completed
this part of our journey. Our smiling guide meets us, and
drapes the white silk scarves of welcome round our necks.

    dawn on Holy Mountain
    apartment blocks of Lhasa
    lit by winter crescent.

Above the map

We park in the lay-by signposted 'Viewpoint'. It's a cold afternoon in December, sunny, with the wind blowing from somewhere chill. Two days earlier it had snowed hard, and our route until now has been between snow-banks pushed to the side of the road by the ploughs.

The sun, near setting, is reflected from the mountains as golden highlights, purple shadows. In the distance we can see the peaks of Skye, and far below us the loch gleams, a flat mirror framed by dark pines dusted with snow. The glen is steep-sided. with the road ascending on the northern flank.

We breathe deeply, trying to inhale the beauty of the scene, until we know we have to leave to reach our destination before nightfall, over the high arch of the Skye bridge. As we turn away we suddenly realise that the loch, from this one point of perspective and no other, almost perfectly resembles a map of Scotland.

> Loch Garry
> in the winter sun
> the whole thing

Odyssey

We had rented a gîte in the Dordogne, in a farmhouse outside a little village called Mouleydier. We had the upstairs flat, and the farmer and his wife lived below. We had taken one of our sons and his then girlfriend, now his wife. Walking to the village that first evening we passed the village hall, where the local band was practising for the Bastille Day celebrations. 'It sounds like a Third World band,' you said, and that's how we still think of it today, fondly, but with a memory of bum notes and dubious intonation. It was a lovely place, but daytime temperatures were in the high 30s, and that definitely affected our enjoyment of the holiday.

All was well at first; we had excursions in the local area, to Bergerac and to some of fortified castles on the Dordogne—Beynac, Castelnaudry, Domme, La Roque Gageac—where English and French garrisons fought each other for control of the country. Then we went further afield, to Rocamadour in the stifling heat, where you had to buy a hat to protect your scalp from the fierce sun. We dutifully visited the shrine of the Black Virgin where I was less than impressed. Then on to Padirac, and the descent of the Grand Gouffre, a massive cave, by cable car.

Our son and future daughter-in-law decided to visit her parents in Germany. They caught a rail connection at Perigueux and departed. On our own now, we made the most of our remaining time. We took the train to Bordeaux, arriving in time to see the Tall Ships just before they set off *en voyage*. The valley of the Dordogne is dramatic, the river taking tremendous sweeps like the Cingle de Tremolat, with deep gorges, overhangs and caves, homes to our early Cro-Magnon ancestors over 30,000 years ago. We had to see the painted cave at Lascaux, and we did, sort of. An artificial cave has been built, to preserve the original from unintentional damage by the CO_2 and water vapour in our breath, and by the bacteria and moulds we may inadvertently take in with us. Lascaux II is an exact replica, reproducing very faithfully the features of the original. It was spellbinding, seeing the representations of bison, wild cattle and horse. Nearby, in the Parc Prehistorique, they are attempting to back-breed the Tarpan, the type of wild horse our ancestors may have painted. They are short, sturdy, muscular beasts.

The temperature continued to climb, and we found a local lake where we swam to cool down. In the evenings you painted, and I read Ulysses. I finished it.

> keeping cool in caves
> going back into the past
> with art and James Joyce

Bastille Day in the Auvergne

The day has started well enough—we have by now completely lost track of the calendar, and don't realise it is Bastille Day. We drive into the village for our morning shopping—bread and wine is really all we need—and find the market in full swing. We buy a couple of little rolls of fresh goats' cheese, and some savoury walnut bread to eat with it. About to head back, and ignoring the funfair set up on both sides of the main street, we hear a samba drum troupe start up. They have heavily painted faces and wear bright costumes, and they seem to be enjoying themselves. The leader has a fine sense of rhythm, blowing on a whistle and delivering the beat with hand and stick. Most of the rest follow him, on big bass drums and rattles. Some of the remainder catch up with the rhythm from time to time and help it on its way, others don't quite make it. An approximate polyrhythm is fine, but without a melody line from voice or instrument, it becomes a bit monotonous and boring, unless you happen to be watching, as I am, a young woman with extremely mobile hips who visibly appreciates that the samba is really all about sex.

After blocking several main traffic arteries, the band leads us down a side street towards the Fire Station, where An Event is to be staged by the local brigade. In Germany, in the village of Boppard Bad Salzig, we once watched a demonstration and entertainment by the local Feuerwehr - the volunteer Fire Department. It had been conducted, as you would expect, with precision and professionalism, in an atmosphere of serious enjoyment. Les pompiers of Champs-sur-Tarentaine, I would have to say, have charm and ineptitude in equal measure. I'd hate to see them tackle a real blaze, and yet I'm sure they'd mean terribly well and argue seriously and loudly over the most logical way of dealing with their problem.

They have run out an extension ladder from a fire engine to an impressive height, and fix three foam-head attachments at various heights. The gallant pompiers don their shiny metal helmets and, with an air of devil-may-care manliness, run up the ladder to their posts. The hoses are switched on and three spouts of foam jet forth. The jet from the lowest one changes from white to a sugary pink froth, while the other two stay white. From the efforts of a junior fireman on the ground, wrestling with a storage tank, pulling on a siphon tube and shaking it, I begin to surmise that the firemen must be trying to recreate the French Tricolour in foam. The junior delivers a final oath to his apparatus, thumps the tank, and shrugs in defeat. The blue foam never appears.

> connecting hoses
> an essential skill to learn
> for putting out fires

Next they extend a long yellow concertina pipe and attach a hose to its end. This, we guess, is a foam generator, which might easily blanket the car park. When all has been connected up however, a thin stream of gently frothing liquid oozes out of the end of the pipe. The fifty-gallon drum is emptied, to a total lack of effect. At the end, a little three year old is the only person in the crowd who applauds, apart from the occasional half-hearted rehearsing tap from the mock South Americans, now almost as demoralised as the embarrassed pompiers.

That evening we dine out in a local village restaurant, and have a really good Auvergnat meal. Afterwards we decide to park back in our home village and have a look round the funfair. Some of the side-shows and competitions are incomprehensible, but the looks of wonder on the faces of the little French children are, as ever, a source of delight. We are about to head back to our cottage when we notice a drift of people moving towards the field at the back of the village hall. We join the good-natured crowd ringing the field in the darkness, and I suddenly become aware that the music coming from the sound system is that of the Jan Garbarek Group, a Norwegian-led jazz band which weaves elements of Lapp, Indian, South American and African music into a unique atmospheric tapestry.

The firework display, when it comes, is very impressive, the effects well synchronised with a kind of symphonic rock background. As I think back to my disbelieving reaction to hearing a Sami *hauk* played in a little Auvergne field, miles from anywhere, to an audience of mainly locals, I am reminded again just how truly civilised the French are. Culture, from whatever source, really means something to them, and it would be wonderful if it meant as much to the other nations in our small and overcrowded continent. There are, after all, much more important things in life than firemen failing to blow pretty bubbles.

velvet jazz, clear night
high notes pouring into the air
before the fireworks

Recording Yosemite

"A photograph is not an accident; it is a concept." Ansel Adams

I've stood in at least one of the places Adams stood, seen what he saw, and tried to capture, in an image, the essence of the place. The photograph I took isn't the sombre, brooding, charged, black and white shot that will adorn calendars and photography books for many years to come. I saw what *I* saw, in colour, tried to frame it in a way that would convey to others the awe that I was feeling at the time, a summer in the Sierras. It hangs in my study, and I look at it every day.

Wilderness, vastness, the accidents of geological processes, and the whims of botany and climate have combined here to create a theatre beyond human imagining. This is a place that could make you want to rush home and create a national park movement throughout the world. That would be a logical response to the natural drama of this landscape. Was that what happened to John Muir?

The valley floor is carpeted with greenery, but until you're up close you don't realise that what you thought were shrubs and ground cover are trees, one hundred feet tall and upwards. Between them, tourists walk slowly, hushed, apart from the children, who regard Yosemite as their personal playground.

I was looking down as I looked around, with the excuse of trying to recognise Beavertail Cactus and Indian Paintbrush. The truth is larger. Like most folk here I was intimidated by the scale of the landscape. Where else can you see a 2,000 foot waterfall shimmering like white lace down the lower part of a 3,000 foot cliff face? Bridal Veil Fall is a good name. Looking up you can lose yourself; the mind slips into neutral, seeing replaces thinking, and contemplation flies out of the window. Your eyes flick from wall to wall, from front to back and side to side, bounce you into the spinning blue above. Scenic overload is a distinct possibility.

The rock, adamantine-hard, is a pale granite, raw and mostly unweathered. Other granites I've seen elsewhere have been used and abused by the world and its weather. They're rusty, worn, and scabbed with vegetation. Not here. These livid vertical surfaces are too steep for plants to have gained a root-hold in the short time since the glaciers retreated. On the dome surfaces, onion-skin weathering has sloughed off giant boiler-plates of crust, geological dandruff, revealing layers of fresh pale rock beneath.

I don't know if I succeeded in my aim; the scale of the place is just so difficult to deliver in small dimensions, but I love this photograph. My heart is in it.

> fresh as if new made
> and bigger than anything
> bare rocks, just bare rocks

Getting there

Flying over the vastness of Arctic Russia I try to sleep, but it isn't easy. Views from the plane's nose camera are displayed on the drop-down screen above my head, and I can see frozen Siberian rivers 38,000 feet below. The largest one visible is probably the Amur, its bends and loops brilliant white against a grey background.

> ice snake far below
> grips the frozen ground
> television scenery

Later I doze, and when I wake we are above the mountains of northern Japan. Further south, and quite unexpectedly, through the cabin window we see the top of Mount Fuji.

> misty ridges
> merge into clouds
> Fuji pokes through

Narita Airport is 60 km outside the centre of Tokyo, so our tour group has a two hour bus journey to our hotel. The city is vast and sprawling, and although we are told the names of the different prefectures we pass through, we can see no obvious differences between them. We drive over the Rainbow Bridge, high above the dockside area and the artificial islands made from landfill. This is a country very short of space.

After checking in to our hotel we go out for a meal in the sound of cicadas, and find the distinctive orange frontage of a restaurant in the Yoshigawa chain. We dine well and cheaply on salmon, thinly sliced beef, miso soup, pickles and rice. In a convenience store we buy mochi cakes—gooey rice flour balls stuffed with sweet bean paste—and a pair of dark sticky confections we don't enjoy so much.

> soft rice paste
> balls on a stick
> sweet glazed but soy-salty

The Nara Road

We drive through tall bamboo forests, and in every hamlet we see persimmon (kaki) trees growing, leaves gone but the large orange fruit still hanging from the branches. There's a saying here (which I've forgotten) about the patience needed to wait for kaki fruit to ripen. Goodness, it's worth it though. The fruits are larger, sweeter and softer than their cultivated cousins, Sharon Fruit, but I don't suppose they crop as well, so they're not commercial. Higher up the hills are groves of *hinoki* trees—Japanese cypress. These have massive straight trunks, ideal for supporting temple roofs, *torii* gates and anything else where strong support is needed.

Our first stop is the Todaiji temple, already thronged with visitors and semi-tame Sika deer begging for the special 'deer crackers' sold to feed them with. They're noticeably smaller than our red deer, and at this time of year the stags are distinctly smelly—maybe they're smelly all year round? The temple is massive, housing a giant bronze statue of the Vairocana Buddha—the Rushana Daibutsu. Beside it is a smaller but very beautiful gilded wooden statue of the Kokuzo Bosatsu—a *boddhisatva*, one who postpones his own enlightenment to help others attain it.

It is raining heavily when we reach the Kasuga Grand Shrine, the uphill road lined with 3000 stone lanterns. A Shinto service is taking place, and we are invited to stay and to observe, watching the priests enter the *honden*—the inner sanctuary—bowing and clapping hands as they do so. Music is playing—a *shakuhachi* flute and stringed instruments, samisen or koto—and a young girl, a maiko, performs a slow, dignified. solemn dance. Her dance represents, no, *is*, we are told, the voice of the god speaking to us through the medium of dance. It is extremely moving, ritualistic and very graceful, as are so many things in Japan.

> the Rain God
> is as necessary as
> the Sun goddess

Skye impressions

All the way north torrents gushed down the hillsides below the snow patches, wraiths of mist float up like cold smoke, a hammering of rain, a blast of water drenching the car, the spillway overflowing from the dam top at Laggan creaming down the sloping front, careening down the curved flow channels at the sides, jets of white water arcing out and drifts of vapour like Victoria Falls clouding the roadway. Safely on Skye the waterfall at Sligachan reminds me of Gullfoss but on a much smaller scale. Houses along the quayside at Portree are painted white, pink, powder blue, primrose, and terra cotta, with one grey stone exception. Clouds massed over the mountains dragging their tails over the hill tops. A larch with its top bent over, cracked by the wind, makes a statement about the power of nature. In the hotel before the bar opens the sound of Miles Davis' *So What*. So this.

> jazz on a summer's day

At sunset a skybreak of blue and gold dispels the grey clouds. In fading light, the tower of the crag above the harbour, headlights of cars on the coastal road. In the middle of Portree Bay a navigation buoy flashes with a seven second repeat. As an earworm the sound of Geoffrey Burgon's *Nunc dimittis* in my head can't compete with Barbra Streisand from the sound system in the bar, but thank goodness that isn't not too loud.

I am wakened by a pair of gulls walking about on the lead roof outside our bedroom window, and look out to a view of the Cuillin Hills, and an early sun touching the colourful quayside houses. Staying away from home I usually memorise shower controls the night before with my specs on, so I can work by touch in the morning. I forgot to do it this time, standing in a cold shower trying to read the out of focus settings. After breakfast I find rhododendrons on the walk to Portree. I'm not sure which species, but it is fairly large leaved, the pink rosettes with deeper throats. I walk round the peninsula overlooking Portree harbour. The tower at the top gives a fine view out towards Stoer, with its grandiose Old Man.

> tap, tap
> bloom, bloom

We drive down to Broadford in the afternoon, but turn back on
the Elgol road because of potholes. One in particular, just
by a cattle grid, is a foot deep, with no way around it, so I
reverse and we go back to Portree for an excellent meal
in the fine restaurant that calls itself a café.

Misty next morning. No clue in the light to say what time it is,
and no sign of it lifting any time today. Everything damp, sodden,
dripping. Mist settles on the grass, turns it blue green. The crags
have near vertical scarps, showing the columnar structure of the
basalt lava flows, each about 30 feet thick. Dunvegan Castle Gardens
this morning. As usual the house is less interesting (to me) than
the grounds. There are some nice plantings; a very good water
garden with two decorative waterfalls and a stream planted up with
Lysichiton, Trillium, Erythronium, some good species rhodies.
Around the garden walls there are now only ornamentals, but it
has a great woodland garden walk. The video in the castle is by the
previous McLeod Clan chief, the one who tried to sell the Cuillins
to pay for his castle roof. I don't remember the details, but some
deal was done to keep the mountains in public hands. The roof has
been fixed and they are now working on the windows. For all that
the McLeods own St Kilda, and there were loads of St Kilda photos
on the walls, I can't find any St Kilda postcards in the gift shops.

> Scottish garden
> North American plants at home
> setting down their roots

Then we drive to the Cuillins at Glen Brittle. Mountains appear from
the constant mist, utterly majestic and threatening my memories.
Did we really climb these peaks? Yes we did. Memory has it that we
climbed Sgurr Sgumain via the Cioch on the Sron na Ciche. I know
we climbed Sgurr a Madhaidh, but we did another peak that same
day and I seem to remember it being Sgurr na Banachdich. I know
we came down one of the peaks via Coirie an Eich, a long walk back.

On another day that week we came down by Tairnealair, so we may
have climbed Sgurr An Fheadhain. A long time ago. Anyway the road
from Dunvegan to Sligachan is wonderful, with amazing views of
Black and Red Cuillin. At Sligachan we walk over to the old bridge,
which was the only bridge there in 1963 when we first visited Skye,
take in the view, and continue up the path for a few hundred yards.

> fear and excitement
> the first rock climb
> remembered

Back in Portree we see the Outer Isles ferry coming into Portree
harbour, and you make up some melodramatic conjecture
for its stopping here, well away from its usual route. We see
someone being transferred to it from Portree pier, but by
the time we've had another delicious meal in the cafe it has
gone. Clouds lift from both Cuillin ranges in the evening,
and I sit writing notes with a glass of wine in my hand.

The person I was in 1963 has completely disappeared. I have
no idea what his ambitions, desires, route maps might have been.
He no longer exists. I've done enough in my subsequent life—
achieved things I couldn't imagine—that it no longer matters.
I have made my own path through life.

> damn Heraclitus
> getting it right
> and so early

The hooded crows seem more sophisticated than their all-black
cousins, but the ravens, my favourite birds, still beat the lot. We
watch a trio of them tumbling in the air, exalting in being able to
do it. Later a single raven in a wind hover, a mist arch over the hills.
The Gathering Ground is a natural amphitheatre, a neat flat circle of
grass, surrounded by basalt walls. An Edwardian poster in a gallery
advertises Highland Games, with a £10 prize to the winning team!

Snow patches in the high corries and in the gullies, and the north facing high slopes. Mist drapes the hills, the seven second flash of the navigation boy a heartbeat in the centre of the bay. Not so hard to understand how much I love climbing the hills, since Skye was my introduction, way back then. Hard to take my eyes off the massif, which I know to be one face of a horseshoe. Lucky for some.

> black ring
> of hard rough rock
> a good start

Le Pigeoniere

Our holiday home in Normandy is a converted dovecot, a circular
building with a small cottage attached. The lower floor area
contains the living room, bathroom and kitchen, the whole of
the upper floor a huge round bedroom. The roof is thatched, and
has a clump of iris growing out of the apex. This is a traditional
feature round here, and practical too, as the outspread roots help
to keep the roof watertight. The novelty of living in such a unique
place is offset by the fact that it is in the middle of nowhere,
overlooking a dairy farm, but three kilometres away from the
nearest village, which itself has few amenities or attractions.

So for the first two days we observe the habits of cows from
our bedroom window as they walk, milk-slung, from field to
makeshift milking shed, which takes four cows at a time. After
that we have to travel further afield to find things of interest.

Such as the Bayeux Tapestry, of course, and the landing beaches of
Gold and Juno, the bombed and rebuilt town of St Lo, the remains
of the artificial harbour at Arromanches; trips to all these and
more fill our days.

We love Honfleur, its pretty harbour, quayside, and the old wooden
church of Ste Catherine's, constructed by boat-builders. It's a town
which might have been made for painters, and we watch an elderly
Japanese gentleman, wearing white gloves and assisted by his
attentive wife, try to paint the scene. We love the Tapestry, seeing
the real thing rather than representations in books. We drink the
Calvados, and the cidre bouché. We mourn in the war cemeteries, all
those young men dead; and think about the fighting in the bocage,
this land of sunken lanes and high hedges, so hard to attack, so
easy to defend. And the civilian deaths in all the villages we passed
through. And Pont l'Eveque, where I miss the chance to buy cheese.
We walk along the Mur Atlantique, among the huge concrete bunkers
and gun emplacements. I swim in the sea, but cannot forget all the
deaths on the beaches. We visit Villedieu-les-Poelles, centre of the

French bell-making industry, and learn all the processes which go into creating them. Why do they use goat hair and horse dung in the casting moulds? We buy a tiny handbell as a souvenir. I now ring it during poetry workshops to mark the passing of time.

And in the evenings we return to our doocot, light the barbecue, eat our supper, drink our wine, and I write poems. At peace.

> a line of heavy cows
> swishes through the tall green grass—
> Normandy butter

Fontestorbes

En route back from Montsegur we come upon a car park with a sign advertising a natural spring, so we stop. The spring appears out of a cave with a wide, high entrance, and we decide to explore. Access is by a curved line of square cut stepping stones forming a crenellated wall, with the overflow gushing through the loopholes to form a waterfall. We walk over it carefully and step into the cave. Beyond the opening it is light and roomy, and the stream widens, running clear over a gravelly bed. The water looks so inviting that you splash my legs with its crystal coolness. We stand in a shaft of sunlight shining through the collapsed cave roof—an open swallowhole. The remains of the roof lie all about us, a jumble of rocks above and below the water level. As I bend to scoop some water to cool my face, I notice that one of the stones we had stepped on a few moments earlier is now underwater. Then I see the water rising inexorably and steadily to flow over another stone. You are at the back of the cave, trying to photograph the circle of blue sky framed by the opening in the roof. I shout to you to come back immediately, and you sense the urgency in my voice.

By the time we reach the wall outside, water is beginning to swirl over some of the stepping stones. We make the last few steps at a rush, and when we reach the roadside we look back to see that all the stones are now under water. The stream has become a torrent, crashing over our route in an impressive waterfall. It is only then that we translate the warning notice into English: "Fontaine des Fontestorbes—Intermittent Spring—Water Level Varies".

> siphon fills and empties
> a beating heart
> in the depth of the cave

Soothmoothers on Mainland

Leaving Lerwick, we drive south to Sandwick and take a small boat across to the island of Mousa. The famous Broch is an obvious feature, a tapering cylindrical tower clearly visible from miles around. The grass is kept bitten very short by a flock of wary sheep. By the path to the Broch, avoiding the numerous sheepish leavings, we see the bright blue flowers of Spring Squill, a small, delicate plant I last remember seeing outside Maes Howe in Orkney.

The broch is a large double-walled construction of local stone, laid without mortar, an impressive piece of workmanship and skill. The gap between the walls is braced and bridged by horizontal stones, and it contains a staircase and recesses for storage and shelter. It's difficult to imagine how it was used when built, but these days it's home and nursery for shearwaters. These far-travelling seabirds make their nests in crevices and gaps in the stonework, coming in after dark to feed their chicks, to avoid predators like skuas, or bonxies as they're known here. Mind you, in the summer here, during the Simmer Dim, it doesn't really get dark at night. We are far north here. At night, I'm told, the eerie calls of the birds echo round the walls.

Further south we reach the tombolo linking St Ninian's Isle with Mainland. It's a curious feature, a narrow spit of white shell-sand forming a causeway to the little island, and flanked by blue sea on either side, where the terns plunge-dive for fish. We make our pilgrimage, as so many others have done over the centuries.

Our last stop today is the archaeological excavation of the Jarlshof settlement, at the extreme south of Mainland. Walking over the exposed foundations of houses, barns and stores for hay and grains, it's possible to imagine the bustling life in this Viking township. Shetland, and Orkney too, were Norse lands before there was a Scotland, and only became Scottish as part of Margaret of Denmark's dowry, in the late 15th century. Most of the landmark names in Shetland are Nordic, like the island names—Yell, Fetlar, Unst. Tystie, the Shetland name for the red-legged guillemot, is the same word I heard in Iceland.

    shearwaters fly in
    after sunset, to the Broch
    Spring Squills bloom unseen

Three temples

Our Kyoto day starts at Sanjusangen-do temple, dedicated to Kannon, the goddess of mercy, known as Guanyin in China and Chenresig in Tibet, in turn linked and with a change of sex to the Indian Avalokitesvara, the boddhisatva of compassion. Confused? Don't be: just think of all the names as personifications of compassion, and you won't go far wrong. We all need compassion.

The grounds of the temple contain box bushes, immaculately spherical, and the temple itself is the longest wooden building in the world. It contains a three-tiered rank of 1001 statues of Kannon. In the centre is a larger carved image, with 1000 arms and 11 heads, one of which is the Amida Buddha. Before each group of statues stand the images of fierce guardians, most of which are derived from the Hindu pantheon. In this place I am overwhelmed by feelings of reverence, my own Buddhist practice being completely in tune with my surroundings.

The Heian Shrine is a Shinto temple and garden, featuring a tea-house, a lake with stepping stones, and all the trees taking on their delicate autumn colours. It aims to suggest nature and to evoke feelings of contemplation and harmony. Works for me. In Shinto, places and objects have spirits—the *kami*—which must be acknowledged, revered and accepted. It's complicated. The majority of Japanese practise both Buddhism *and* Shinto, shifting naturally from one set of beliefs to another.

Today's final temple is Kinkaku-ji, the Golden Temple, deservedly famous. It rises from, and is reflected perfectly in, a large artificial lake. In the lake are man-made islands, shaped like turtles, each crowned with a group of pine trees. Real turtles, looking nothing like islands, swim in the lake. There's a dry garden with raked grey sand, and a 600-year old pine, trained to grow from a horizontal trunk. A place of ceremony and celebration.

> three gardens
> two religions
> rooms and reflections

Perseverance

Climbing Suilven, fat, unfit, out of practise in the mountains, is
probably not a good idea. It's a young person's game, hillwalking,
like the day before's poet finishing his climb in time for lunch.
But when I start something I like to finish it, black chair or
no black chair, even if it becomes a struggle with myself.

The new boots are a mistake. They rub behind my heels, raising
blisters that burst, stingingly, but they are indeed, as advertised,
lightweight, so my feet carry them along the many miles of track.

At first the mountain seems to get no closer, but it's a
beautiful thing from any angle, the strengthening sun
turning its distant grey ramparts into many layers of purplish
Torridonian sandstone. At the fork, where the Canisp path
continues, I turn off, gaining height at last. A boggy lochan,
girded by black peat and white quartzite boulders, is circled,
then the enormous wall of the mountain looms above.

Halfway along the base a stony path towers upward, to the pass, the
bealach, between Suilven's twin summits. This incredibly steep path,
mostly of loose rocks, twisting and turning, takes me two hours to
ascend but, thrawn as I am, I manage it. Through a gap in the tall dry
stane dyke bisecting the saddle, I stubbornly continue. From here
the northern path to Inverkirkaig is obvious, a narrow brown thread
weaving far below, between the mossy hummocks and wee lochans.
A scramble up a steep rock pitch opens on the airy whaleback ridge
of Caisteal Liath—the Grey Castle—and the mountain's true top.

The rewards for this persistence, this doggedness, are many.
The stunning and unique views from the top are themselves
worth the effort. The whole of the top left corner of Scotland is
laid out before me. Assynt's ring of inselbergs—Cul Mor, Cul
Beag, Canisp, Quinag—each rears up in isolation from their
flat ground of Lewisian bog. The blue Atlantic contrasts with
the white shell-sand beaches of Clachtoll and Achmelvich.
Almost, but not quite, below me, yellow gorse gleams along the
track to the Lodge, and its lochan sparkles in the sunshine.

But I have gained far more than vistas from my obstinate walk.
It has strengthened my determination to overcome obstacles.
I spare a few minutes in meditation, then eat my cheese
sandwich, drink my tea, and begin the descent.

Retracing my steps, stumbling at times, staggering and tripping from
tiredness, footsore and with legs aching, I climb down the path and
trudge along the track to the Lodge. Nine hours after setting out,
I return, take off my bloody socks, and stretch out in a hot bath.

> sound of a cuckoo
> coconut scent of gorse flowers
> up and then down

Northern barbarians

Hadrian's Wall was built to protect Roman Britain from the attentions of its rowdy northern neighbours. The Great Wall of China was intended to save the Chinese Empire from Northern Barbarians. The Danube was a natural barrier, reinforced by garrisons of Legions to halt the advance of Huns and displaced Goths from the north. So what is it about the peoples of northern lands that frightens the folks down south?

I have to declare an interest here. I'm from further north than some, but further south than others. I was born in Edinburgh, which puts me firmly in the northern half of these islands, but to the Highlanders I'm a Sassenach, a soft southron nyaff; to Shetlanders a soothmoother. But my ancestors were from Aberdeenshire, in the north-east of Scotland, but south-east of the Highland Boundary Fault, a major geological junction where two profoundly different geological terranes were welded together. Aberdeenshire is not Highland, but Lowland. Gee, Officer Krupke, no wonder I'm a mess! Genetically, I'm probably a Pict, so my ancestors might have been among the ones doing the marauding, reiving and pillaging which upset our southern cousins.

Does it make me more aggressive, more uncivilised, the fact that I live in the lands of long summer days and interminably long winter nights? What insurrections, rebellions or invasions do we plot in our northern fastnesses, where the wind howls round our castle walls, and the rain steadily fills the buckets we've laid out to catch the water dripping through our leaky northern roofs?

And yet I remember, one cold December evening, setting out to visit friends, and stopping by the roadside as the northern sky, my northern sky, shimmered and shone in the unearthly green glow of the Northern Lights.

It's maybe more barbarous here, but there are compensations.

build your fortress walls
but we're not barbarians
we're just different

Section III

Capturing the Castle

The caves below Hawthornden Castle are passages and dwelling chambers carved out of the solid sandstone. They are known as 'Pictish', but that's probably a romantic fiction; there's no reason to believe Pictish people ever settled in this area. The earliest record folk in the Lothians are the Godothin, whom the Romans called Votadini, and they spoke Brythonic, a variety of Old Welsh, as did the Picts. Maybe that's the connection, the tribes who named a local settlement Penicuik, and a local hill Caerketton, both names recognisably Welsh-related.

It's a dwelling suitable for an extended family, and one chamber has blackened walls indicating hearths or ovens. There's also a small hole in the floor with access to the cliff outside, probably used as a latrine. In another passage the wall has been carved into a grid of square recesses forming a doocot, perhaps to supplement the castle diet in earlier times.

Chambers and passages bear thousands of pick marks probably made by the short double-ended picks miners often used to open seams of coal. The stone here is soft and easily worked, but even so it must have required a considerable effort to create this warren for cave dwellers. It reminded me of the similar underground chambers at Gilmerton, in Edinburgh, and a 'troglodyte village' in the Loire Valley on a 'Cycling for Softies' holiday (it wasn't soft at all). The rock is very solid, with no obvious joints or faults, ideal for building, as long as it is harled with mortar or pebble-dash to protect it from weathering.

Back in the Castle courtyard there's another underground room below a metal cover. It's called a bottle dungeon or oubliette, but again there's no evidence it was ever used for prisoners. The room has a 'garderobe' in a corner. As well as being used as latrines, garderobes were places to hang furs and skin coats, the ammoniacal vapours protecting them from the attentions of moths and other pests. The name evolved to become the English 'wardrobe' and lost its lavatorial connections.

My room in the Castle is named for the great Lithuanian-born poet, Nobel Prize-winner Česław Miłosz, for whom I feel a kinship. I know his poetry, and I have seen the high regard in which he and other poets are held in Lithuania.

> empty cells
> below the Castle
> the birds have flown

Mes ♥ Poetas

The flight from Amsterdam to Vilnius is made lively by a group of
Belarusian or Ukrainian workers well fortified with brown paper
bags concealing bottles of Jägermeister and red wine. They pass them
round among themselves in a manner less and less circumspect
and more and more noisy as the flight proceeds. I've never drunk
Jägermeister as I've always, perhaps mistakenly, equated it with those
other medicinal-tasting European liquors—Enzian from France,
Bečerovka from the Czech Republic, or Unicum from Hungary.
We had tasted Enzian, flavoured with gentian root and reputed to
be the cure for all known human and animal ailments, in the hills
of the Auvergne, where the plant displays its magnificent yellow
flowers in the high meadows. The locals say they never drink it neat,
but only mixed with pastis, and then not very often. So of course
I had to try it. My verdict is that it's only one notch below toxic.

The plane and its noisy passengers lands safely at Vilnius airport,
where we exchange euros for *litas* and meet up with our guides.
We walk round the picturesque Old Town (there's always
one, isn't there?) and I buy a belt to replace the one I forgot
to retrieve from the security gate in Schiphol. Then it's time
to join our driver and a minivan full of poets from Australia,
Georgia and Latvia. It's a three hour drive from Vilnius to our
cabins at Alausyne, outside the provincial city of Utena.

The next morning, breakfast is eggs and bacon, served with tomatoes
and cucumbers. We were to see many more cucumbers in the days to
come. Then we leave for our tour of the Anykščiai region, in the bus
with its 'Mes ♥ Poetas' sticker in the front window. It is fascinating
to compare this landscape to that of my native Scotland. Lithuania
is a land of lakes and forests. Farms are grassy clearings in the dark
conifer woods. There's always water here; storks patrol the ditches and
lake margins hunting for frogs and fishes. We don't see fenced fields,
and cattle and horses are tethered to stakes, grazing neat circles in the
meadows. The cows are milked *in situ* by old women carrying stools
and pails. A third of the population, including many of the young

men, have left Lithuania to seek work in other EU countries. We see small hand-dug plots for vegetables close to the wooden farmhouses.

The bus stops to pick up more poets, mostly Lithuanian, including my translator, Sonata. She had translated three of my poems into Lithuanian, and they would be the only ones of mine to be read during our tour. In retrospect, I could perhaps have chosen other poems, but that is now water under the bridge.

Speaking of water, we stop at Romuva for an open-air picnic which includes the hallowed but very recent tradition of the poets washing their feet in the very pretty river. There are a lot of biting insects, and I don't escape their attention.

> mosquito's high whine
> silent bite of horseflies
> both take their blood toll

Getting a big hand

Our caravan of poets from Lithuania, Latvia, Georgia, Russia and
Scotland set off for our first reading in the open air at Debeikiai, with
a charmingly earnest local girl playing accordion in the intervals. My
poem here is a long one about the concentration camp at Terezin/
Theresienstadt. It goes down surprisingly well; one elderly member
of the audience is in tears as he shakes my hand. Then fourteen of
us pile into an 8-seater minibus and drive to Anykščiai and the local
church outside which we'll be reading. We are joined by a group of
young people in what I guess to be Tudor period costume—well,
the Baltic equivalent, what do I know? On the church steps they
perform the very formal and elegant dances of the times, to our
obvious and heartfelt enjoyment. There is one hilarious moment
when the dancers are interrupted by a wedding party emerging
from the huge church doors, but wedding guests, priest, dancers
and audience all laugh and applaud, and the dance restarts.

After the readings and the inevitable speeches, all the poets are
crowned with traditional midsummer oak leaf wreaths, and very
fetching we all look. We leave for Niuronis and a 'Museum dinner'
in a restored farmhouse with earth floors and a wood-burning
stove—not much chance of running out of wood in this country.
The food is truly delicious, sweet pickled Baltic herring, hams
and sausages, and smoky little potatoes baked in the embers, with
slightly sweet butter. Lots of toasts are drunk in good Lithuanian
vodka—*denktina*. When we get back to Alausyne I discover I
can't take off my wedding band because of an insect bite.

The next day we travel to a bee museum before our reading in
Ignalina. It is a fascinating place, with magnificent carvings of
ancient bee deities. The museum curator is licensed to conduct
weddings, and we are delighted to watch one taking place.

On the Sunday morning our guide takes me to a pharmacy in
Utena to get something for my insect bite, which shows no sign
of getting better. We are reading in the open air at the Antanas

Miškina house, and I have a lump in my throat when I see the Scottish Saltire flying beside the flags of Russia, Lithuania, Latvia and Georgia. Patriotism can strike when you least expect it.

The final reading is in the local library in Utena. By now my whole hand and wrist are so swollen that I can't even wear my watch. The organiser agrees that she and her daughter, who speaks excellent English, will take me to the hospital after the reading. I am given intravenous and intramuscular shots of antihistamine and antibiotics, then we drive to the cabins for our farewell party, where, sadly, I'm not able to drink the vodka.

En route home, in the terminal at Schiphol, I finally manage to slip the ring off, and the swelling immediately starts to go down. I arrive home at midnight, in time to pack for two days of poetry workshops in Elgin and Buckie—quite a contrast.

> vodka and friendships
> honey beer and mead
> a flag is not a country

Hawthornden run

On a dreich, damp October morning I leave the castle wearing singlet and shorts, and start running up the long drive to burn off some calories. The trees, tall and majestic on sunnier days, fit a mood of autumnal triste. Branches still in the windless air, they stand limp, leaves imperceptibly yellowing. Running under the canopy I am occasionally struck by falling leaves and heavy drips from the earlier rain.

There's a lot of variation between trees in their reactions to the deepening autumn. The big ash tree outside my window loses its leaves quite quickly, but they will stay green until they fall. But the ash keys which festoon the branches, have turned from green to yellow. When they deepen to brown and dry completely the wind will shake them down. A larch far below in the gorge has dropped all its needles, and is now a forlorn tangle of brown twigs. The birches are yellowing, as are the sycamore leaves, pirated with black spot fungus.

I run past a short avenue of Irish yew, stripped of their pink juicy berries by blackbirds and thrushes. The seeds are extremely toxic, but they pass straight through the birds' digestive systems protected by a layer of mucilage. The oaks are smothered in acorns, an exceptional crop this year, and it's also a Mast Year for the beeches.

At the top of the drive I turn on to the road and pound along the pavement passing a field of jacketed horses, and hedgerows where ivy is still flowering luxuriantly, the sickly, tainted-honey smell still attracting the last wasps of the season. Soon they'll form the hard little black berries the song thrush enjoys.

It's a great year for the birds. Jays are feeding on the acorns, other birds are gorging on rowan and hawthorn berries, rosehips and elder. By the time I reach the first houses and turn round to run back, my mood has turned too.

it's that time of year
when all the clocks
in all the trees change

An interpretation of dreams

Mostly, I can't remember my dreams, but I wake some mornings aware that I must have been dreaming. Maybe a couple of residual images leak into the space reserved for conscious thought, but the longer I fail to focus on these images the quicker they fade.

Unlike psychiatrists, professional or armchair, I don't attach any importance or significance to the content of dreams. Sorry, but I don't think they mean anything, and they never have. They come, I suspect, from an area I'll call random access memory. When awareness shuts down in sleep, the brain itself doesn't stop working—it can't. Systems for blood flow, oxygen delivery and cell maintenance continue to work. They have to, otherwise we'd be dead. And these systems include the workings of synapses, those fuzzy connections between nerve cells which mediate the electrical signals travelling along axons and dendrites.

Memory stores are part of the least understood features of our complex brains, but the pathways must be similar to those in better characterised areas such as the sensory and motor systems.

During sleep, levels of neurotransmitters, the chemicals which activate synapses, are lower than when we're awake, but there are still some drifting around in the blood stream, released in response to varying hormone levels.

So I can build a conceptual model of brain activity in which a pulse of chemicals, deep in the night, randomly opens connections between memories which wouldn't normally be connected, suggesting unreal events, imagined histories. The illogical and often bizarre results come up on our inner display screens.

There's only one category of my dreams that sometimes has a slightly longer persistence. That's recurrent dreams, the ones I might have, with novel variations, maybe once a month or so.

A recent example is the workplace one. In it I haven't retired, but I'm back where I was, doing the same job, but as an unpaid volunteer. As if that would happen! Apparently I've been doing this quite happily and successfully for some years, unknown to my colleagues, but I've decided it has to end. The new layer last night, the dream within the dream, is that I clearly saw, on my office desk, several saxophone mouthpieces, including one that could tune itself. The origin of this one is easy to see: I've recently bought myself a tenor sax, and I'm teaching myself how to play it, fulfilling a long-held dream.

'Round Midnight
blowing
like a dream

Sharks and surf

Green sea surges over the rocks at the harbour mouth. The rocks are pseudo-sedimentary, with an appearance of bedding. Thin pale planes separate the darker, thicker members. Hot fluids, released by rising plumes of molten granite, penetrated the very fabrics of the rocks, altering their minerals and crystal alignments. When formed they were on the raised limbs on either side of the ascending granite batholiths, baked like clay in a potter's kiln, and squeezed by the weight of long-gone mountains above them, then bathed and simmered in hydrothermal fluids until they were done.

Along the roadways, under the shelter of the high hedges, there's a huge diversity of plants—campions, honeysuckle, briars and brambles, and many more. The verticals are provided by foxgloves and the feather-heads of grasses.

I'm going to return to the question of a 'spirit of place'. What does it really mean? Maybe familiarity has something to do with it. If there's something which characterises a type of landscape that we recognise, and with which we associate specific feelings, whether of comfort, joy or dread, then on re-encountering such landscapes, our feelings return. This reinforces the associations and strengthens our identification. Let me give an example: If I reach the top of a mountain, I will have a feeling of achievement, strengthened by an enjoyment of the view from the top, of being in the highest place in that particular area, and seeing things that are unique to that place, to that experience. Later, all mountain-tops will have similar feelings and memories associated with them, and I will want to recapture them. So I do it again. Once bitten, twice bitten.

Then again, if we've experienced fear in the dark depths of a cave, we'll always associate dark narrow places with feelings of claustrophobia, with fear of the unseen.

Here's a possible childhood memory:

From a cliff-top at Penzance, I look down on the sea. A basking shark is swimming past the headland. The memory is conflated with a memory of my father taking us out on the sea in a rowing boat. I think from Oban. I remember looking through the clear water, seeing swirling kelp, imagining some scary water creature rising up from the unseen depths, tipping us out of the boat. Ever since then I've been scared of getting out of my depth in the sea. So reading Norman MacCaig's poem about the basking shark I can picture myself in that scenario, drifting on a tin-tacked sea surface, with unseen things lurking in the depths. But the feelings I have are very different from the ones Norman expresses in his poem.

I don't honestly know if I invented the memory, but I when we came to Cornwall this year, you for the first time, me to re-visit, I want to go back to the place I remember. But when we get there the cliff isn't the one in my dream; it looks totally different, and I couldn't possibly have looked down from that one and seen a shark. We explore up and down the coast, crossing off cliffs, 'Not this one. Let's try ...' and it isn't until we go to Mousehole that some kind of uncertain recognition occurs. If it did happen, it probably happened here. The topography is right.

> smugglers' havens
> narrow moorings, hidden coves
> wreckers, rovers, rogues

Newquay is different. It caters for the mass market holiday, and looks to provide what that market wants. Maybe it's just me, but it's not what I want. Away from the town, however, the natural beauty of the beaches and the sea are stunning. I love the way the sea colour changes from grey to blue, depending on whether it reflects cloud or open sky. The Atlantic rollers charge in, pursued by a westerly gale bearing occasional scuds of drizzle. The bigger waves bear passengers, surfers who swim for the leading edge, stand up and glide in, some sliding sideways, or doing acrobatics, before falling through the breaking surf.

Yesterday, off the cliffs at Lizard Point, I watched two Grey Seals swimming, diving for fish just at the side of a kelp bed. That was a good day. We had started by visiting the china clay mine at Wheal Martyn, then we drove to a tin mine near Helston. The old mine workings were intact, and the experience was a lot less gimmicky than, say, Derbyshire's mines and caves. Our guide was knowledgeable, and happy to answer our questions. These old mines, hand hewn, follow the contorted lines of the original tin veins, taking us on a turning and twisting journey, up, down and sideways. Many of the walkways were on metal grilles suspended over the mine floor, which was often a flowing stream. No wonder Trevithick invented his steam engine here, to pump water out. The workings would be flooded within days if the pumps ever stopped.

don't go down the mine
Daddy, don't go down the mine
have a swim instead

The Madagascar Blues

This stretch of road is dead straight. It leads from the nature reserve
we've just left to the distant blue hills ahead. In the middle distance
a small town sprawls in a nothing-special area. Everyone walks
everywhere here, so it's no surprise to see lots of women walking
along the roadside, children shouting, 'Cadeaux, Cadeaux,' as
we drive by, and men pushing iron-wheeled carts, heavily laden
with firewood, charcoal and produce, or driving zebu cattle.

White-painted bungalows on the outskirts are surrounded by
strong walls, railings, and barbed wire. Black-shirted guards with
guns lounge in the door- and gate-ways. Our guide advises us not
to photograph them, and we nervously comply. The main street is
lined with sapphire shops; armed dealers man stalls, and the sellers,
faces daubed with red mud against the fierce sun and biting insects,
walk among them with small twists of cloth holding their finds.

A river, red like all the others in this region, flows under a bridge in
the centre of town. The red earth banks on either side have been cut
back so much that a large pool has formed. Here people wade, waist-
deep, panning the mud for grain-sized gems. At the sides, where
the water is less silty, women wash clothes, then spread them over
bushes to dry, as we've seen elsewhere on the island. Upstream men
work new cuttings, surrounded by huge heaps of red earth waste.

The workers are local people, drawn here by the hope of
finding big blue stones to make their fortune, but the only
ones who make money are the dealers, the middle men, who
buy cheap and sell to the big corporations. These men are all,
or nearly all, foreigners, outsiders. The income from sapphire
mining doesn't stay in Madagascar; it bleeds away offshore,
like the money from oil and the beautiful rosewood forests.

> rainy season day—
> red river cuts through forest
> washes out blue stones

Gathering storms

Storms can excite us, but they also remind us just how powerful natural forces can be. No matter how much we think we can control our world, they tell us our control is limited. High winds wreck forests and buildings; hurricanes and typhoons flood fields and towns; storm surges devastate coastal communities, and lightning strikes cause forest fires. And they kill; the loss of life may be just a few, or it may be thousands.

The autumn gales that roar through the treetops in woods, scattering leaves and twigs to the four corners, can make a woodland walk exhilarating. Who hasn't kicked up leaves and watched the wind catch and carry them? As long as it stays dry it's great fun. Rainstorms are less pleasant, but sometimes it's good to stay indoors, looking out at lashing rain or seeing hailstones jump in the grass outside. We don't deal with them so well if we're obliged to venture forth though. Walk through a city street after a storm, and you may see dozens of broken and discarded umbrellas. Our little machineries of protection aren't all that effective when wind combines with rain. Then there are the hats blown off and sent to that far-off place where lost hats wander, headlessly.

Living by the sea, the storms that are most spectacular are ones driven by the strong north-easterlies we usually get in winter. The waves are piled up by the long fetch of the wind, and come ashore along our north-facing coast. Ally that to a high spring tide and you have the recipe for a storm surge, a mound of water forced into the gape of an estuary. They can travel quite far inland, unless stopped by rocks, seawalls or vegetation.

If the peak of one wave meets the trough of another, they cancel each other, lowering the height of both waves. But when peak coincides with peak, they are both reinforced, producing higher waves. Because of the geometry of our local beach, wave refraction leads to some places being favoured spots for giant waves, when an incoming sea meets another ebbing back from

the beach. This results in huge spikes of water being thrown
20 or 30 feet in the air. And I've seen big waves hit the seawall,
sending the sea clean over two-storey houses, the weight of water
breaking off a roof gutter on the inshore side of the houses.

Then there's the seafoam. Rarely, but often enough it seems, a
storm will churn up offshore seaweed, breaking down its tissues
so the alginates are released, creating a stable mousse which the
wind picks up, plastering rocks and houses with a layer of spume.

I never tire of watching the power of the sea, while knowing
it is eating back the land, smashing rock against rock, pebble
against pebble, suspended sand grains inexorably wearing
away whatever barriers we create to defend ourselves.

> gale force nine forecast
> a ten will keep us indoors
> the spray in the air

Smack dab in the middle of nowhere

The bus pulls in to Barstow, between Las Vegas and Los Angeles, in heat not much different from that which we'd experienced in Death Valley a few days earlier. The town is home to a huge outlet mall, full of designer brand shops. To some in our company that is a happy prospect, the chance to shop, and at bargain prices. To me, sadly, that is just no attraction at all. I get no pleasure from the shopping experience. Online shopping might have been created with people like me in mind. See what you want, click on a button, and wait for the delivery person—it's a boon and a blessing. It minimises transactions, so it's my preferred purchasing strategy. I don't want to be confronted and confused by choice, variety or decision-making. Show me what I want, what I really really want, and let me acquire it quickly and without effort or stress.

In Barstow I move from one air-conditioned aisle to another, peering in shop windows at objects I neither need nor desire. I can't wait to board the bus and move on to our next stop.

But the town has more to it than meets the tourist eye. It was established at a railroad junction, where two lines met. That was its whole *raison d'etre*, a place where goods and people came together briefly, before going their separate ways again. And so it became a nexus for those seeking work or hoping to hide from the law, creditors or other pursuers in the terrible years of the Great Depression; a stopping-off point for hoboes hoping to jump freights or hitch lifts.

And the graffiti scrawled on fences and walls by bored or desperate optimists seeking onward transport was the inspiration for a wonderful piece of music, 'Barstow', by the lyrical hobo composer and musical instrument inventor Harry Partch.

> O, you lucky women!
> Why the Hell did you come?
> Jesus was God in the flesh.

Walking the Wall

Some world famous tourist attractions can be a disappointment, but I have to say that the Great Wall of China is anything but. It is, in the true sense of the word, awesome. We climb the steep section at Badaling, not the 'soft' side where VIPs and the less fit ascend, and I make it to the top. Much of this section is extremely steep, and very steepest sections are near-vertical steps. At times this feels more like hill-walking than just walking.

It is very cold at this altitude, with some ice on the slabs in the shadiest corners, and a biting wind. People are slipping and falling regularly, but thanks to the strong grip of my shoes, I don't have a traction problem. Despite being constantly pestered by vendors—'Rolex! Gucci Bag!'—it is exhilarating. I feel a tremendous sense of achievement when I reach the fort on the summit ridge. The views are superb from this height. For mile after mile, *li* after *li*, the Wall stretches on, following the ridges. How much effort did it take to build this wall? How many workers did it take? How many died? What purpose did it serve?

The plains below, once the regions of the 'Northern Barbarians' are part of China now, and one of the northern peoples, the Manchu, invaded across the Wall, overthrowing the Ming Dynasty, setting up the Qing Dynasty, and moving the capital to Beijing. So it wasn't a total success as a defensive barrier.

Coming down is occasionally tricky. At one point I trip on my own walking pole, and a young Chinese girl grips my elbow to catch me and steady me. I am met with many smiles and much warmth here and elsewhere in China. Many are curious about my long white beard and silver hair. They seem to think I'm a real ancient, like one of their sages. Little do they know.

> climbing the Great Wall
> I breathe the cold winter air
> in good company

River and canal

The Bund in Shanghai is beautiful. I like the Victorian and Edwardian buildings, although I can't imagine what life must have been like back then, in the Concessions—districts ceded to Britain, France, Germany and other countries. We walk along the Huang Pu river, which joins the Yangtze a few miles downstream. Back on the bus, we go to the Yu Yuan Garden, a really beautiful mix of plantings, rocks, buildings and water, the four elements of the classical Chinese garden. The Moon Gate, the Dragon Wall, and the sculptures of mythical creatures intrigue us. I see a painted scroll bearing Chinese characters in one of the buildings, and I ask our guide what it is. He tells me it's a poem by Li Bai (Li Po), one of my favourite poets. We buy gifts for our grand-daughters in a little shop in the garden, where we encounter a couple from Edinburgh! Then we walk out into the narrow streets of the bazaar area. We buy rice paper, silk scarves, and T-shirt for our grandson. I never pay the price asked, but haggle it down until it's agreed. The salesperson shows me figures on a large calculator, and I gesture my responses, shake head or nod. Somehow we communicate, across the differences in language and culture. I am given a chit which I take to the kiosk to pay the cashier. By the time I come back with the receipt my purchase is wrapped. Walking through the bazaar, one of our group has her camera stolen from the pouch on her bag. It is unzipped and taken without her being aware of it. While she goes to the police station with our tour guide, the rest of us are taken to the Shanghai Museum, which is small, modern and very tasteful. I am hugely inspired by the furniture and, above all, by the Chinese paintings. We buy postcards, a print, and a notebook for calligraphy. After dinner we drive to the Bund for a breathtaking night excursion on the Huang Pu. The coloured lights and displays on the Pudong skyscrapers on the opposite bank makes it one of many breathtaking spectacles in China, probably the most breathtakingly spectacular place I've travelled to.

Our last full day in China starts with a drive to Suzhou, the 'Venice of the East', but which city isn't the Venice of Wherever? Remember St Petersburg being described as the 'Venice of the North'? No need to compare really. Suzhou is a city criss-crossed by canals. So is St Petersburg, so is Venice, so what? We have a leisurely boat trip down the Grand Canal and a lesser canal, both extremely picturesque. The deckhand keeps bringing out boxes of goods to sell us—postcards (no), coolie hats (definitely no), tiger balm ointment (certainly not). The white marble bridges are very pretty, and waterfront life is obviously popular—we see people doing their washing from the steps outside their back doors. A walk on the city walls next. What is it with the Chinese and defensive walls? Is it something that reflects a national insecurity? Believe me, they've nothing to feel insecure about—they impress the hell out of me. Anyway, there is nothing special about this one, except maybe the Water Gate with its sluice and portcullis. Back on the coach, we drive to the silk factory, where the processes of silk manufacture are demonstrated. I didn't know that sometimes there are 'twin' cocoons with two pupae. These cocoons produce silk which is too 'flossy' to be used for silk thread making, but which is ideal to produce membranes to make silk quilts. The filament isn't spun, but is cleaned and stretched to form a web the size of a face cloth. When dried, it is stretched further by hand to form a rectangular sheet, and 64 of these sheets go to form each silk quilt, which is marvellously light, but warm in winter and cool in summer. We also find out that the caterpillar droppings are used in Chinese medicine, and that the dead pupae go to make 'silk products' for the pharmaceutical industry—gels, mousses and lotions etc. Nothing is wasted. I like the sign reading 'Don't take the cocoons.'

> silk threads are pulled
> from cocoons, spun together
> eight threads per fibre

Back to Suzhou City for a visit to the 'Master of Nets' garden. It isn't really to my taste; too many rocks and buildings, not enough plants. Bits of it are very pretty, though, and it's been given Unesco Cultural Heritage status. We finish the day at the Embroidery Research Institute. This is a real surprise to me—I hadn't honestly been looking forward to it all that much—but the embroidery work is just staggeringly beautiful. My favourite is a large double-sided piece with a lion on one side and a tiger on the other—goodness knows how that was made.

Traffic in Shanghai is the worst I've ever encountered, apart from that caused by the tram works in Edinburgh city centre.

> shopping in Shanghai
> no abacuses in sight
> just calculators

Fieldwork

I became interested in primate behaviour as an offshoot of independent studies of palaeoanthropology, our origins and evolution. I read voraciously on the subject, some years before my formal studies in ethology in the 1970s. For lemurs there was Alison Jolly's book; Jane Goodall researched chimpanzees, and there were several scientific texts on monkeys. But the book which interested me most was George Schaller's study of the ecology and behaviour of the mountain gorilla. I know that humans are closer to chimpanzees than to any other great ape, but I find gorillas fascinating.

During the course of his 18 month fieldwork he studied gorilla groups in the Virunga Volcanoes area, a triangle where the borders of Congo, Rwanda and Uganda come together. 'His' gorillas became used to him, eventually ignored him, and resumed the normal behaviour which had intrigued him from the start.

They live in small family groups, several females and young, with a single silverback male. When young males reach maturity they leave the group, living on their own until they can form their own families with other females. It's a form of behaviour common to many other mammal species, ensuring stability and avoiding in-breeding. Perhaps the Hapsburg monarchy in Spain should have tried it. Their predilection for cousin marriage almost certainly led to the high frequency of genetic disorders in their family.

Schaller followed the groups every day, observing them rise in the morning, feed, interact, play, move around their territories, and build nests each evening. The lighter animals make nests in trees, but silverbacks are too heavy. He identified their food plants, even tasting them to see what attracted gorillas to particular plants (most were quite bitter). His study, widely read, was influential in creating a research base for study and conservation, and to the founding of a national park and an ecotourism industry.

His subsequent studies were on deer-tiger interactions in India, the

Serengeti lion, the chiru antelope and clouded leopard in Tibet. What impresses me most is his meticulous and dedicated fieldwork—I've read extracts from his field notebooks. I like fieldwork too, but at least with geology the subjects don't try to run away or hide from you. Rocks stay still, especially if you hit them with a hammer.

gorillas in mist
tigers in the deep forest
an eye for nature

Visiting relatives

Seeing a dwarf mouse lemur feeding on sap in the Madagascar rainforest on a wet night with thunder crashing all around is one of the highlights of the trip. The animal seems totally unconcerned by the torches of the local trackers and the fourteen British tourists gawping at it. It is feeding at about head height in a young tree just off the road. We are all mesmerised by this small mammal with big eyes, one of the group of animals we'd come this far to see. Rainwater drips from the leaves, runs down our jackets and splashes on the pot-holed road, but we don't mind a bit. The night-time expedition is on our first night in Ranomafana lodge, on our way south from Antsiraby.

The prosimians—lemurs, lorises and tarsiers—have always fascinated me. There must have been a common ancestor of them and the monkeys (which gave rise to the apes, including us), so it's tempting but wrong to think that our distant ancestors must have been like them. That view misses out the dimensions of time, geographic isolation, and evolution. Living lemurs are as evolved, as specialised, as living monkeys and apes have become, over the millions of years that separate us from the common primate ancestor.

A couple of days later we stop at a wildlife reserve and, after picking up a different pair of local trackers, we set off into the forest, picking our way among unfamiliar trees and plants, avoiding thorns and stinging plants, and protected from insects (we hope) by daily liberal applications of *Deet*. We are walking quietly, as advised, when our guide stops and points to a tree much like all the others we have passed. But this one holds a family group of ring-tailed lemurs, some feeding on leaves and berries, other stretched out resting or sleeping. I've seen them in zoos before, but there is nothing like seeing an animal in its native habitat, behaving naturally. A baby clung to its mother, looking over her shoulder at this strange group of visiting primates taking pictures.

> pointed faces, long tails
> but grasping hands
> just like us

Origins

Where did it all start? Oh, I know the Big Bang is literally the defining moment for the whole universe and, closer to home, my birth was the beginning of yours truly, but I'd like to know where our species started.

The trouble is that fossilization is a random and imperfect process. We can look today at other living primates and clearly see that our species belongs in this group. What we can't usually see are the intermediate steps, the points at which we and our other immediate relatives shared common ancestors before going our separate ways, undergoing separate development. There are rare fossils which might be fairly close to being our ancestors, which have characteristics we think ancestral forms might have had. But we can't be certain.

And then we have fossils which are evidently related to us in some way, but which have died out, leaving no living descendants. It's not a neat 'Tree of Life', but a thicket of twigs and branches. Human nature being what it is, we like to have clear-cut pictures of linear progression, from small brain to large brain, from quadripedal to bipedal, from living in the trees to the grasslands, from fruit eaters to omnivores, from cooking to culture, farming to cities. But these are vast simplifications of changes which took millions of years to accomplish, and the evidence is geographically scattered, sporadic, incomplete, and often hard to date precisely. It's a jungle out there.

In broad-brush terms our lineage goes from ape-like ancestors through *Australopithecus* to early *Homo*, and from early *Homo* to us. In each of these broad stages there is a bewildering plethora of scattered bones, names and interpretations, and we're not close to achieving consensus.

And there is always the unexpected, like the discoveries of the Georgian *Homo erectus* fossils at Dmanisi, the tiny sub-species of *erectus* from Flores, and some recent discoveries of creatures like *Australopithecus sediba*, which possess a mix of primitive

and advanced skeletal characters similar to what we'd expect
to find in a true intermediate, but not quite the whole set.

where do we come from?
which set of African bones
shows our ancestry?

Mythical beasts

Mythical beasts are very common, although you don't see them very often, in the flesh I mean. But images on canvas and as sculptures are all around us. The world is made untidy by them. But what do they signify? Why have we created them? What purpose do they serve?

Maybe they start as something used to frighten children into doing something they don't want to do? 'Wash your face, or the Bogeyman will get you.' But you've never seen a Bogeyman, and none of your friends have, so you imagine one. You project your worst fears onto some kind of representation you can see in your head. Or some 'helpful' artist will create a picture of their own worst imaginings, label it 'Bogeyman', and then you're stuck with that image, sharing a myth with everyone else who's seen the same picture. Having viewed Hieronymous Bosch's *Garden of Earthly Delights* up close in the Prado, I'm sure he must have had a terrible childhood.

At other times, our desire to create powerful beings who can bring about magical transformations in our lives results in wonders like Godzilla, King Kong, Santa Claus. It's a reflection of our limitations as human beings that we imagine only supernatural creatures can bring us the fulfilment of our dreams.

The unicorn was such a magical beast. To the casual observer it may appear no more a variety of horse with a long horn and a weakness for virgins, but only its body is equine. Look closer. The chin wears the long beard of a goat; the cloven feet—not horses' hooves—are those of a deer, and the tail is that of a lion. Let's be up front, boys and girls, that is one weird creature, to be seen at its wondrous best in the tapestries at Cluny.

The phoenix is another one. This'll get you: What kind of bird do you know self-immolates, rises from its own pyre and goes off to perform miracles? Not your familiar blackbird or robin, I'll wager. In fact it's not even in Audubon. There's a beautiful bronze statue of one in the Summer Palace garden in Beijing, flanked by two more mythical creatures, the dragon and the *qilin*. The dragon, the common four-clawed kind and the five-clawed Imperial species, are seen ubiquitously in China. The qilin (pronounced chee lin) is rarer, but very interesting. He's a sort of butch unicorn, a protective creature and a harbinger of spring. Throughout China, lion sculptures are very common too, but their features are so stylised that they might as well be mythical.

Strange, how myths are sometimes more powerful than reality. Me? I'll believe in unicorns when I see one.

> where's the unicorn?
> deep in the mind's dark forest
> symbol of goodness

Up Pompeii

I was born in Edinburgh, a city with a volcano in the middle
of it. Maybe that's what started my interest in geology. Naples
too has its volcano, Mount Vesuvius, but it's an active one,
whereas Edinburgh's Arthur's Seat last saw action in the
Carboniferous, more than 300 million years ago. Vesuvius
has affected Naples' history and the attitudes of its people. It's
an intense place, with vivid colours, great beauty and great
squalor, great riches and great deprivation, a city of contrasts.

Its last eruption was in 1944, and the scar of the main lava flow is
still visible from the top of the mountain, the rim of the crater. No
doubt it will erupt again, whether with an explosive event like that of
AD 79, or a relatively quieter effusion of lava such as its most recent
eruption. From the crater there's nothing to base a prediction on.
There's a patch of sulphur-stained rock emitting steam, but that's
about it; there are no clues to what's going on below the surface. Of
course it's continuously monitored by scientific instruments detecting
seismic activity, ground inflation and gaseous outputs, and an early
warning system is in place, with regular evacuation training exercises.

There was no such system in AD 79. Pliny recorded a shaking of
the ground, continuous thunderous rumblings, loud explosions
and a cloud 'resembling a pine tree' coming out of the mountain.
In northern Europe, 'pine tree' suggests *Pinus sylvestris*, but
Pliny meant the parasol pine (*Pinus pinea*) which was so familiar
to him. Its shape is nothing like the Scots Pine, but resembles
a mushroom cloud. Huge volumes of volcanic ash and pumice
rained down on Pompeii, while pyroclastic flows, red hot clouds
of ash, lava fragments, steam and other gases, charged downslope
at great speed, engulfing the settlement at Herculaneum, both
now incorporated into greater Naples. Many of Pompeii's
inhabitants had left their cities a few years earlier as a consequence
of a disastrous earthquake but had returned and were buried,
asphyxiated or burned by the ash. With hindsight it's likely that
the earthquake was a precursor of the eruption which followed.

The area today, with much of the two cities excavated by archaeologists, and now tourist hot-spots, reveals fascinating glimpses of the ways of life of their inhabitants. But nearby there's evidence for continuing volcanic activity. Near Pozzuoli, at Campi Flegrei, you can walk on hot ground that sounds hollow when you drop rocks onto it; there are numerous fumaroles emitting steam and sulphurous gases, and pools of boiling, bubbling mud. There's a magma chamber, and you know it's far below your feet, but it does make you nervous. And out in the Bay of Naples there is evidence for huge collapsed craters—calderas—which speak of enormous eruptions in the past, far larger than anything Vesuvius could ever produce. Africa is still moving, colliding with Europe. Southern Italy and Sicily are the regions where the cracks are showing.

> smelly yellow rocks
> cooked in the Inferno
> sold to tourists

The rocks remain

We're on an arc of islands, simmering in a shallow tropical
sea. Lands to the north and south have sundered, torn apart.
In between, our ground slumps as the planet's plates pull away
from each other. The seas, milky with plankton, teeming with
fish and all that feed on fish, flood in to cover sinking swamps.
Shellfish and shrimps burrow in the limy mud. Each small
island has its coral tiara, its fringe of wave-splashed reef.

Every so often the ocean shimmers, as the rising heat triggers
earthquakes. Most are small tremors, as stresses adjust. Sometimes
a locked fault unlocks itself in a huge pulse of energy. These
major destruction events trigger vast earth movements and can
create ocean waves that ripple outward from the site of failure.

Heat from the rift zone raises semi-molten rock upwards, punching
faster through conduits as it rises, becoming more liquid, pooling
in a churning magma chamber, building pressure. At the surface,
all the volcanic pyrotechnics light the night sky. The supporting
acts in this variety show of geological force are fumaroles of
sulphurous steam, fire fountains, and fissure vents. The headline
acts are the big volcanoes, blasting pulverised rock, steam and
gases through the lightning storms, high into the stratosphere, or
oozing vast lava flows. Lava flows are known by two Hawaiian words
according to whether they are ropy or blocky, pahoehoe or aa.

It's a violent place, our world—nowhere is safe. But that was
then, a long time ago. Things are quieter, cooler now, in the place
where I live. All that's left are solidified lava flows, eroded dykes
and sills, and ash-fall tuffs studded with old volcanic bombs,
like raisins in rock cake. The congealed pipework remains on
show—Bass Rock, the Law, the mushroom head of Traprain.

> somewhere far away
> floods, earthquakes, big eruptions,
> nature's shock and awe

Ice and fire

The mid-ocean ridges are places where the deep-sea floor spreads apart through the injection of molten magma, heated by convection currents in the Earth's mantle. As the new rock cools and solidifies, it pushes against the old oceanic crust on either side, widening the oceans by a couple of centimetres each year. That's about the same rate as your fingernails grow, so it's not exactly high speed. These are the constructive margins of the Earth's tectonic plates. Far away from the oceanic ridges, the distal margins of the plates collide with other plates, crumpling and folding, causing earthquakes, producing volcanoes, and sinking below continents in subduction zones.

In the 1950s and 1960s depth and seismic data were used by Bruce Heezen and Marie Tharp to produce the first reasonably accurate maps of the ocean floors, and they showed some totally unexpected features, including ridges extending along the centres of all the world's oceans. In profile, the mid-Atlantic Ridge gradually rises on either side of the centre, then a steep-sided central valley, the Rift, shows where new lava is erupting, where the plates on either side are moving apart. Most of these processes take place out of sight, far from land, in the middle of the deep oceans. There's one place—Iceland— where the ridge breaks surface, and we can travel there to observe the effects of one of the Earth's planetary scale phenomena in action.

It's a unique place, a cold land in a cold sea, which freezes round the edges in winter, but it has underlying heat which pours out lava, provides hot water and power to its inhabitants and results in some amazing scenery, as the American and Eurasian plates move apart.

It's April when we land here, and the temperature is a headache-inducing −5 C, dropping to −9 at nights. Despite this, some of the locals in Reykjavik's main street display a reckless disregard for the cold. We put on as many layers of clothing as we can, and venture forth on a tour bus, stopping to admire a line of snow clad craters, remnants of a fissure eruption. We are awed by the Gullfoss waterfall, where a river flowing from a glacier plunges into a deep cleft, making a right-angle turn as it does so. The vapour from the fall rises like steam into the air, freezes and condenses on the river banks and the sides of the gorge.

Geysir, the place which gave its name to geyser phenomena world-wide, is no longer active, but its neighbour Strokkur is energetic and spectacular. We stand at a safe distance from a pool of boiling water, but still close enough to feel the heat on our faces, until a giant blue bubble rises from the depths and bursts, sending up a tall plume of water and steam. And then, twenty minutes later, as the siphon deep in the hot rocks fills and boils once more, raising the pressure in the conduit, it does it again.

We travel to the Blue Lagoon, then relatively undeveloped, where waste hot water from a geothermal power station is discharged into a settling pond, taking on a pale blue tinge from suspended silica particles. It's a weird experience to swim in this warm water as the snow falls on our heads.

On the central plateau we see, in the distance, one of Iceland's large volcanoes, this one quietly puffing steam into the clean cold air. Years later we would experience the effects of a large Icelandic eruption, when Eyjafjällajökull erupted, sending up an ash plume which trapped you in Germany with the family, and forced us to miss a planned trip to Puglia.

A Thingvellir we stand on the edge of the American plate, looking at the distant edge of the Eurasian plate. In between, Lake Thingvellavatn, and the buildings which mark the site of Europe's first democratic parliament. At this point our tour guide, talking about her pride in Iceland's democracy, has tears in her eyes, and I decide that I like these folk. As long as they don't sing folk songs, first in Icelandic, then in German, then in English.

> snow on the black rocks
> Viking sculpture by the sea
> whooper swans swimming
> looking at autumn trees here
> thinking of a treeless land

snow gently falling
a swim in warm blue water
geyser blows off steam
a meeting place by a lake
the land where Earth splits apart

Xenophobia

Sometimes things that don't belong here have grown so familiar that they look as if they've always been here. If they're plants, we label them 'alien species'. But that's an insult to the inalienable purpose of seeds to do what evolution designed them for, to produce more of their kinds. Most will die out, unable to cope with whatever natural conditions prevail in our ecological neck of the woods.

Trees are an example. The ones 'native' to Scotland came in as the last ice ended, starting around 10,000 years ago. So birch, oak, hazel are definitely native, as are pine and juniper, probably holly and a few others. They were the pioneering woodland communities. But climate has varied over the millennia; we've had warm spells when more tender species from further south were able to establish here. Then, as conditions swung the other way, they died out. So elm, lime and beech became native, then alien, all without them being aware of it.

The most problematic introductions have been manmade. We travel, we see plants we like, and we say, 'I'm having that,' so Douglas Fir, European Larch, flowering currant and rhododendrons become native in the enclosures we call gardens and parks. That's mostly fine; I'm happy that I don't have to travel to San Francisco to see an avenue of Giant Redwood. I can go to Benmore Garden to view a fine example.

It's when they spread outside their designated plots that things go wrong, and sometimes on a huge scale. The west coast of Scotland is smothered by *Rhododendron ponticum*, whose deep cover shades out all other plants. By many riverbanks Himalayan Balsam, a pretty flower but seriously thuggish, out-competes our native species. Japanese Knotweed was introduced as an ornamental plant in gardens, but it spread like wildfire, and it's very hard to kill. The forestry plantations of Sitka Spruce are unnatural and gloomy places where our native wildlife can't find a home.

It's the same all over the world. I've seen eucalyptus forests in Madeira, with the native laurels in decline. Prickly pear was introduced to Australia, and they had to bring in a Mexican cactus moth caterpillar to control it. Kudzu vine is a serious pest in America. So my Japanese maple grown from a Tokyo seed, and my ginkgo from Kyoto are going to be tended and admired, but I'll keep my eye on them so they don't escape.

> native woodland trees
> the ones which grew up with us
> the natural way

A square and a garden

It is raining when we set off for our visit to Tian'an Men Square and the Forbidden City, but it stops, leaving us in thick mist, so we can't see much detail in the Square. The building housing the Great Hall of the People is enormous. Mao Zedong's mausoleum isn't exactly an attraction to a western tourist, so we give it a miss. It's a bit ghoulish to think of his twice daily journey in the lift from his freezer up to the refrigerated glass case and back down again. We wander around, taking photos of Chinese tourists, children waving red flags, and quite happy to be photographed. We, particularly me, are stared at by several Chinese people, and sometimes they want to take my photograph. It's the white hair and white beard. For some reason, the Chinese retain their dark hair long past men of my age in the west. Not for the last time in China I am assumed to be much older than I am.

The entrance to the Forbidden City is at the far end of the Square, guarded by two huge stone lions and below a giant portrait of Chairman Mao. The male lion has a globe under his paw, the lioness a cub—that's how you tell them apart. Nine is the most propitious number in China, and really important doors like these have nine rows of nine brass studs embedded in them. Then we are through, and into the complex of buildings and spaces that is the Forbidden City. There is nothing like this anywhere else in the world. From here, 24 Emperors ruled China for nearly 500 years, until Mao proclaimed the People's Republic of China in 1949. The last Emperor (Pu Yi) lived here up until 1911. The power of the Emperor was absolute and unquestioned. The largest building in the complex is the Hall of Supreme Harmony, roofed in yellow tiles, for this was the colour only Emperors could use. There is a canal, the Golden Water, which curves in a shape resembling the jade belts worn by officials. At various points there are huge bronze cauldrons, which were kept full of water in case of fire.

The Imperial Gardens are at the far end of the Forbidden City. Avenues of ancient trees face beds of colourful flowers, and there are several pavilions and water features. No garden is complete without rocks, water, buildings and plants. There is an amazing rock garden, the Hill of Accumulated Elegance, surmounted by the Imperial View Pavilion. The rocks come from Tai Hu Lake and have astonishing shapes carved by water and wind. There is a sign in front which reads 'A single act of carelessness leads to the eternal loss of beauty.' I like that.

We move to the *hutong* district for a quick rickshaw ride. The hutongs are the old courtyard dwellings popular in Beijing until recent times. Now the majority prefer to live in flats, and most of the hutongs have been demolished, with a few preserved for the benefit of tourists like ourselves, who find them 'quaint' and 'ethnic'. Walking through the alleyways is an obstacle course, with all the street sellers trying to sell us stamps, cashmere, Rolexes and other fake tat. But somehow we survive. The park contains a section with exercise equipment for the elderly, which is something I'd like to see in British parks. Why should kids have all the fun?

A word about Chinese dragons, which you see everywhere. Only the Imperial dragons have five claws. Your average domestic dragon must make do with four.

> no tanks in the Square
> unless hidden by the mist
> but the dragons roar

Vodka

I mixed myself a Bloody Mary, but I didn't have anything to stir it with, and I couldn't be bothered going to look for anything, so I just gave the glass a little shake. It didn't mix the drink properly and when I took my first swallow the nearly neat vodka, lying on top of the tomato juice, caught the back of my throat. I was instantly transported back all those years to a hotel bar in St Petersburg, or Leningrad as it then was, drinking unstirred vodka and tinned orange juice. I remember how the oily, peppery liquid brought the tears to my eyes, until I could shake round the ice-cubes and blend the mixture into some kind of drinkable smoothness.

We'd flown in from Glasgow to Pulkovo Airport that morning in an Aeroflot Tu-154, sipping 'Soviet champagne' in plastic cups as we flew over Finland's lakes, then past a twenty kilometre smoke-plume from a huge peat-burning power station. It was your first ever flight. That evening we were in a 'hard-currency' bar, where only dollars or sterling were accepted. It was illegal for Russians to own hard currency, so the out-of-place guy in the corner of the bar, an obvious Russian in an unfashionable shiny blue suit, had to be a KGB plant. Banal balalaika and male-voice choir music filled the bar, alternating with 'rock' singers. It can be truly bizarre when people are singing their hearts out and you can't make out a single word. They are clearly feeling deep passions but if you don't know their culture or language these passions are totally meaningless to you—they could be singing about a lost love or a lost sheep and you wouldn't know the difference. Customers had to shout over the din to make themselves heard, so I doubt if 'Boris' was able to gather much intelligence from the bunch of Scottish tourists in the hot and smoky room.

After the first vodka and orange I switched to tasting, neat, the flavoured vodkas: *Limmonaya*, really lemony but sweet with the sharpness; *Pertsovka*, with paprika, good and warming, and my favourite, the Bison Grass one—I never did discover what the flavouring was. At the end of the evening, fed up with the noise, we walked upstairs towards our room, but on the way we discovered another little bar. The upstairs bar was smaller, much quieter but if anything hotter— the outside temperature was 32° but inside it must have been over 40°. I remember at one point seeing an elderly American trying to buy currency, not realising he and the potential sellers could have been jailed if blind eyes hadn't been turned. My own were rather affected by the high-octane hooch I was imbibing.

> as a young barman
> vodka was my main tipple
> drank a lot of it

Most of our group were just your average Scottish tourists, gawping at everything, complaining of sore feet in the Malachite Room of the Hermitage, photographing each other in front of the repeatedly-stormed gates of the Winter Palace. "This is Rembrandt gallery," said our Intourist guide. "We have thirty-four Rembrandts in collection, but just thirty-one on show presently." I was staggered. Thirty-one Rembrandts all in a row! But that's how they were, just stuck in rows in what appeared to be a random sequence, or maybe they were arranged by size, I can't quite remember now. I prefer to see his self-portraits hung chronologically, so you can see the progression from brash, confident youth to frightened and questioning old man. The fear hits him when the money goes, and his family starts dying—it's all there in that touchingly lumpish face, with the hurt and hunger in his eyes.

St Petersburg is a beautiful city, waterways lined with pastel stucco palaces, each a similar height, making for a very level skyline broken only by the enormous gilded dome of St Isaac's Cathedral, and the wonderful gold spike of the Admiralty building in the Peter and Paul Fortress stabbing into a cloudless blue sky. Down the Neva River the marvellous Peter's Palace—*Petrodvoryets*—reached by hydrofoil, was a strange mixture of chopped grass lawns, stunted salvias, and beautiful gilded statuary, stunning in the sunshine. Trick fountains splashed only the deliberately unwary, but they still managed to raise the only laughs we saw on Russian faces.

Moscow was definitely a lot less beautiful. We dutifully toured the Kremlin, GUM, and the Novodevichy Monastery, the University and the Eternal Flame. In the Space Pavilion we saw their cramped and heavy space stations - a lot of low-tech brass screws held things together. One of our group wondered rather disapprovingly how it was that the Russians could launch men into space, but couldn't provide egg cups for our breakfast bowl of boiled eggs in the hotel. Not like Glasgow at all.

> Gagarin's space suit
> rows of vehicles, capsules
> major achievements

One man in our party didn't appear to be a conventional tourist with the 'SovScot' group. He was a young Scots-born American who had earlier been in the US diplomatic service in Moscow. He'd come back on the quiet to meet a Russian girl he'd known before. She joined us on the bus in Sochi, on the Black Sea, for a trip into the Caucasus, and they spoke in Russian all the way. I remember the word *protektivny* being repeated several times over the tea and fruit bread at the Dagomys tea plantation, and finally figured out it meant condoms. Just over the Georgian border we stopped for lunch in the Abkhazian town of Gagra, scene of a lot of shooting in the Georgian civil war. Soup was ghastly; half an inch of violently coriander-flavoured grease sitting on top of a reddish liquid, with lumps of unrecognisable meat floating in a sour-cream and cabbage broth. Burnt lamb shashlik followed, washed down with a revolting orange-red sticky wine which tasted like cough mixture.

We drove higher, into the low clouds, which obscured our view of the mountains and the beautiful (it was said) Lake Ritsa, where Stalin had his holiday dacha. It was a place where he could entertain his friends, drinking copious amounts of vodka until the tears flowed. Theirs, not his.

> borscht brought out the worst
> vodka kept Party going
> Georgia on my mind

Some grand canyon

A river has cut a deep gorge through the soft sandstones at this point, but it's not the river I can see from my window—the North Esk. That's a gentle stream, flowing from a source in the Pentland foothills to join the sea at Musselburgh. This stream doesn't have the cutting power to gouge a 50 metre deep gash in the landscape, between the gently rolling fields, woods and farmlands on either side.

That other river was a much bigger, more boisterous torrent, escaping from the snouts of glaciers as the Ice Age waned, probably the result of the collapse of seasonal ice dams allowing huge volumes of water to drain from temporary lakes ten thousand years ago. Perhaps some ancient hunting band from the first settlers witnessed the cataclysmic cascade of water, ice, boulders and rock flour scouring its way downstream, finding the shortest route to the sea. More likely not. Geological surveys can determine the probable sequence and extent of events, but placing humans in this landscape is speculative at best, romantic tosh at worst.

Gravity is the force behind river flow, and rivers usually cut deepest close to their sources, where the gradients are steepest. So the glacier front which spawned this river probably wasn't too far away. The canyon sides, precipitously steep, provide an ideal microclimate for trees to grow, and this glen is thickly wooded. Some of the specimens I see from my Castle window must be 30 metres tall. Native species predominate, but there are several fine, tall alien conifers towering over their oak, ash and birch neighbours.

Where exposed, the sandstone walls, home to jackdaw and peregrine, are a pleasant pale pink colour, often massively bedded. This stone is itself the remains of a much earlier river delta, Devono-Carboniferous in age. In places it shows excellent examples of sedimentary structures, such as cross-bedding, pebble horizons, and 'fining-upward' sequences. And of course such a regular and well-cemented sandstone forms an ideal building material. Hawthornden Castle, and Rosslyn Chapel, in their several building phases and restorations, are made from stone hewn and dressed in this very spot.

rising river mist
wraps around the trees below
the breathing forest

Temples and taxidermy

Coming in to land at Xining is interesting, seeing the dissected spurs of the Tibetan Plateau. The stewardess announces it is zero degrees at our destination, and you say, 'Zero degrees? If it's raining it'll be snowing.' It isn't snowing, but there is a bitterly cold wind blowing outside the airport. We are driven to a restaurant for an excellent dinner. A big group of local Hui Muslims are celebrating a wedding, a birthday, or whatever. The men, in dark jackets and immaculate white caps, sit at two tables, while the women and children sit at separate tables. On so many levels this is just plain wrong, but how do you say that without causing problems? All I know is I couldn't live like that. I'd have to pretend to be interested in cars and football, and I'm not sure I'd be believed.

The hotel is in the main city square, where the Han Chinese dance in the open air every morning at 7am. We decide against having an early start to observe them. However, as we are dozing off to sleep, you notice the sound of rain from the bathroom, and we discover water coming in through the ceiling and pooling on the floors of bathroom and hallway. After some discussions and translations, we are moved to another room.

The Kumbum Monastery at Ta'er Si is crowded when we arrive, with Tibetans praying in each of the many temples. They do this every day in pilgrimage season. There has been a light dusting of snow overnight, and it is extremely cold. There is a large *chorten*, a Tibetan 'stupa' at the entrance, and an impressive row of eight more just inside. Stupas are large dome structures both commemorating and symbolising Buddha or some saintly individuals—here it's former lamas. The pilgrims each make a circuit of the chorten by prostrating themselves, sliding forward face down on knee pads, and with outstretched hands protected by wooden blocks or thick gloves. Then they stand up and move forward, prostrating themselves once more, until they have completed the circuit. Others are spinning prayer wheels, fingering prayer beads or mobile phones, and chanting. Most of the pilgrims are Tibetan, but I notice some with Nepalese and Mongolian features.

Buddhist pilgrimage
to Qinghai monastery
the power of faith

We start our visit in the Lesser Golden-Roofed Hall, whose
courtyard is bizarrely decorated with stuffed deer, yak skulls, and
other animal bits gazing down at us from a balcony. The pilgrims
bring offerings of money and yak butter, for this is the monastery
where monks make painted yak-butter sculptures, colourful but
incomprehensible, The sculptures are made by hand from the
butter, keeping it from melting by immersing it in ice-cold water.
This, as you can imagine, ruins their hands permanently, so they
can't do this work for long. The sculptures are then painted, and
decorated with gold and silver leaf. The spirituality of the place and
the people impresses me considerably. I turn each wheel in the row
of big prayer wheels—clockwise, of course. The monk on the door
at the Prayer Hall isn't going to let me in at first, not understanding
that I'm a Buddhist, but an offering of money and a bow to the
Buddha get me waved through. I join a line shuffling round the
interior, in the pungent scents of yak butter, people and incense.

Some of the pilgrims here stop in their tracks and stand directly
in front of me, staring at my face. I feel I've been given permission
to study their faces in return. It's a long drive to Qinghai Hu, the
largest salt-water lake in China. Our lunch in a freezing cold
restaurant (The Lake Qinghai Local Performing Restaurant) is
interesting. We have to keep our coats on as the place isn't heated,
and the food congeals as soon as it hits our bowls, so we don't
linger. Outside, some local women display animal skins, shawls
and souvenirs for sale. Their children beg from us, and when we
give them the sweets we bought earlier for this purpose, they and
their mothers are very disappointed—they wanted money. Then
we stop by the lake to take photographs. It is now bitterly cold,
and the lake is beginning to freeze. A mixture of salty slush and
drifted snow edge the sandy shore, but the beauty of the place is
awesome, surrounded by snowy mountains. By the road we stop
to photograph a mixed herd of sheep, goats and *dzo*, the cow-
yak hybrid more common than pure-bred yaks. (Dzo is another

good word for Scrabble and Bananagrams—feel free to use it.) There's a curious offshore structure visible from the settlement, and we can't work out what it is. It isn't until we arrive home that we discover it's a torpedo testing station. How banal is that?

circles of prayer
in the old monastery
winter is coming

Orkney's mysteries

The Orkney ferry leaves from Scrabster, the port of Thurso,
and sails in good weather over the Pentland Firth, passing
the hilly island of Hoy with its eponymous Old Man, and
the spectacular cliffs of St John's Head, at nearly 400m among
the highest vertical cliffs in Europe.

We arrive in Stromness, the Hamnavoe of George Mackay
Brown, and join the bus for Kirkwall. Scapa Flow is an immense
central sea ringed by the islands of Hoy, Mainland,

Burray, South Ronaldsay and Flotta. It was the main anchorage
for the British Fleet in two World Wars, and the place where the
German High Seas Fleet scuppered itself after the surrender.

We are both fascinated by archaeology, so our visits to
ancient sites feature heavily on our trips. Standing stones are
so evocative, always making me imagine the lives of their
builders, and wondering why they were built. They clearly
mark the sites of important ceremonies, but there's usually
no evidence for their purpose, or how they were used.

But standing among the stones at Calaneis on Lewis, or here at
Brodgar, it's impossible not to speculate. I want to know more. Of
course I walk round the Ring, touching the stones, but they tell me
nothing. I look across to the Stenness Stones, to the burial mound
of Maes Howe, and try to work out the meaning of their geometry,
but there is no-one to tell me if I am on the right lines. In the long
narrow isthmus between Loch Harray and Stenness Loch, recent
excavations have unearthed an immense and complex ceremonial
site predating Stonehenge and the monuments of ancient Egypt.
But what was it for? What did people do here? Who were the
people who built these things? Why did they build them? The
winds blow over the green grass of Orkney, but carry no answers.

no trees at this place
stone quarried, cut and lifted
a ring, a dumb ring

Sumo

I wish they'd broadcast sumo again. It was cult viewing, a
minority interest, for a year or so, and it had me glued to the
screen, often with my eldest son. I got to know the rituals,
the rules, the etiquette and the personalities on the circuit.
Our TV set in those days was quite small, and reception was
very poor, but I found it compelling viewing, helped by a very
knowledgeable English commentator who had settled in Japan.

The two contestants enter the ring, the *dojo*, dressed only in loin-
cloths. They throw salt in the air as a gesture to the kami, the
spirits, stamp round the central 15 ft diameter ring, then bow to
each other—always respect your opponent. Then they get down to
business, legs wide apart, hunkered down, heads facing forward,
centres of gravity lowered. They stare intensely at each other for a
long minute which seems longer. It occurs to me now that this is
exactly what many male animals do in the course of their mating
rituals. The staring is at the heart of the conflict, before the serious
struggle begins. Bears do it, tigers do it, elephants do it. Stags
practise a variant, the side-by-side strut, but it serves the same
purpose. You are assessing your rival, and asserting your fitness,
your strength, your confidence in your ability to overcome. The one
who looks away at this point will usually be the loser. It's rivetting
and compelling behaviour, whether in nature or in the dojo.

Then they both stand up, turn round and squat down again briefly,
before the real action starts, fast but never furious—these men are
controlled. They are allowed to hold each other only by their belts.
The aim is to make your opponent touch the dojo's clay surface with
any part of their body other than their feet, or to force them out
of the central circle, over the silken rope which marks the edge.

These chaps are big, seriously big, living in groups in the compounds
of their sponsors, eating huge meals of high-protein food—the
famous *chankonabe*—to bulk them up, and having training
and massage sessions daily. Weight is an advantage, but it isn't

everything. Muscle strength, stamina, speed of attack and clever tactics often beat a heavier man. My favourite sumo wrestler of the time, Chiono-fuji, often seemed slight compared to opponents like The Refrigerator, but his speed and technique were wonderful to watch. Usually he had won the match beforehand, with his stare.

top-knot still uncut
after many tests of skill
violence with grace

Pottering about

Today we will talk about centring. To be centred is to be at a point of balance, to be where the pressures are all equal, so that none can overcome. Centring in the philosophical sense is a thing which goes way back, and it's rooted deeply in Japanese culture, before Buddhism arrived there. Look at a Sumo wrestler—the good ones are so centred they're like rocks. If they had three legs they'd be tripods, and no-one could topple them. But they have two, and therefore can be over-balanced. So keeping centred is a dynamic thing. They move their buttocks back and squat down, their lighter torsos forward, so their point of balance is directly over their tree-trunk legs, ready to move quickly in any direction, or to hold a stance against battering odds.

It's the same when you use a potter's wheel. First you have to centre the clay. You start by throwing a ball of clay onto the centre of the moving wheel. Wetting your hands, you hold the clay firm against one hand and push in with the other hand. Then you push down with one hand on the top, and move the other in again and up. When you take both hands away you should have a smooth cylinder of clay, spinning without wobble or eccentricity of movement. It takes practise.

When you slap the clay down hard on the wheel it forces any trapped air out, so it sticks better to the wheel. It also lowers the centre of gravity of the clay, so it's more stable as it spins. You do the same thing mentally when you're centring. You empty your mind of extraneous thoughts—it's meditation in action, a harmony between mind and body. Getting down.

It's a long time since I did any pottery, but I remember it so well. Using the wheel seemed such a natural thing, shaping a spinning lump of clay to make that first bowl, the first jug, the first vase, the sense of achievement. The feel of the clay in your hands is pleasurable; let's be frank, it's sexy. And without the potter, the clay would just sit there forever, being a soft, wet lump of sticky earth, going nowhere.

> on a stormy shore
> flat pebbles don't move so much
> waves shift rounded stones

Standing guard

China is an extremely mountainous country. You don't appreciate exactly how mountainous until you fly over it on an internal flight. This one is from Beijing to Xi'An, the Imperial capital for 2,000 years, and now the capital of Shaanxi Province. Ridge after ridge of arid hills all look very grey until we come in to land, when we encounter the Yellow Earth of the loess plain, a soil consisting of very fine particles. The yellow colour is from staining by the iron mineral limonite, and the soil is very subject to dispersion by wind and erosion by gullying. The Yellow River gets its name from the huge quantities of sediment suspended in it.

We have a fascinating visit to the Archaeological Institute, and it is a real privilege to be allowed to handle some of the objects dug up in the last two years; trivets made of bronze, and beautiful tricolour glazed earthenware. The archaeologist who shows them to us asks us to guess their relative ages, which is difficult. Then we are whisked off to the Great Goose Pagoda, where I am able to pay my respects to the Buddha in a small chapel within the temple complex. There are three large bronze statues of the Buddha, surrounded by 18 disciples. The little garden in the street leading to the pagoda is colourful and full of exotic flowers.

At our restaurant in West Lake Park that night the dinner is disappointing; the service is poor and some menu items are missed out. They are still serving our meal when we should be outside watching the fireworks. Our guides, anxious not to lose face in front of their foreign guests, are furious with the restaurant staff, arguing angrily with them, but apparently nothing can be done. Instead we have a beautiful night-time walk through the grounds of the Tang Palace Gardens, and we ask one of our guides to sing for us, which makes her feel better.

Next day we see, through the pollution haze, the substantial artificial hill which covers Qin Shi Huangdi's tomb. Qin was the first emperor to unite the whole of China from the four major provinces which had existed before. The hill has not yet been excavated, but is believed to contain a map of the Empire, with the rivers made from mercury. A geochemical survey has found mercury at toxic levels in the soil on top of the hill, so the story may well be true. It is also believed to contain the tombs of 48 concubines, who were buried alive. The whole complex took 36 years to build, and 700,000 people were involved in its construction. Many of the workers were killed, to prevent the location of the tomb from being disclosed. So it remained unknown until it was discovered by accident in 1974, when four local farmers dug up the first broken pieces of pottery from one of the Terracotta Warriors. When we visit, one of the farmers is himself on display in the Visitor Centre, signing copies of the guidebook.

The scale alone makes this place one of the most impressive human monuments anywhere in the world. Three pits have so far been excavated, containing over 7,000 life-size Terracotta Warriors, as well as horses, chariots, birds and animals. The Warriors were in pieces when found, and they're still being patiently restored. It's easy to predict that there will be more wonders to be unearthed here. Even here, half a world from home, we heard unmistakeable Scottish accents behind us, and meet up with two compatriots. The Banpo Neolithic site is interesting, but after what we've just seen it is an inevitable anti-climax. In the evening to a colourful theatre show celebrating the Tang Dynasty. The period is, to me, one of the cultural high points in Chinese civilisation.

> a song from Toni
> to chase her blues away
> on No Firework Night

For the birds

From our cottage in Claddach Kirkibost we can see the beach, and beyond that, on a good day, the Monach Islands, low-lying and now uninhabited, a sanctuary for seals and seabirds. Walking down to the sea I cross a boggy field, unintentionally disturbing some nesting peewits, so I keep my visit short. I notice a nest with two speckled brown eggs in it—they normally lay four. In the afternoon we meet up with a couple of old friends from Dunbar, who have now settled on North Uist. The novelty of us meeting in this remote place is delightful—proves it's not really remote after all.

Our goal next day is the RSPB's Balranald Reserve, and we manage to walk all the way round it. The variety of birdlife is astonishing, including nesting Arctic tern, curlew and oystercatcher. A corncrake is grating away from a clump of flag iris, but we can't see him (it's the male who calls). Among a large group of birds sifting seaweed on the foreshore we identify purple sandpiper, turnstones, dunlin, redshank and sanderlings. Offshore a Great Northern Diver fishes, while Arctic skua, gannets and kittiwakes fly overhead. The wildflowers are just beginning to open—mountain pansy, thrift, goldilocks buttercup and many more—we have arrived too early in the season.

The following day I walk some miles along the road in a wind strong enough to blow my hat off. As I walk I think about the Tokaido and Kisokaido roads from Edo (Tokyo) to Kyoto, successive capitals of Japan in the Shogunate period. This road isn't really like either, but I feel almost like a wandering pilgrim in this landscape, so different from the familiar ones of home.

Later, on the way to Lochmaddy, we stop at Langais Wood. There's now an interpretation board featuring the project Alec Finlay and I had worked on twelve months earlier, and it's strange but gratifying to see my own name in the acknowledgements. I do belong here. It's good to come back.

> only near the ground
> in the cup of a bird's nest
> shelter from the wind

Sensational

Our knowledge of the physical world is derived through our senses, traditionally five in number: sight, hearing, touch, taste and smell.

Sight depends on our ability to detect photons, the packets of energy which form the electromagnetic spectrum. By convention, the continuous spectrum is classified by wavelength into a range which goes from very short (gamma rays) to very long (radio waves). We call the range our eyes can detect the visible spectrum, although other animals can sense higher wavelengths—bees see in the ultraviolet—or slightly lower—some snakes work in the infra-red. We too can sense the infra-red, as heat, through special nerve cells in our skin.

We sense vibrations in the air as sound, transverse waves formed by alternate compression and rarefaction of air in the direction between a source and a detector. Wavelength determines the pitch of the sounds we hear, and amplitude, the height of the wave, its loudness. Our hearing range doesn't catch very high frequencies, which bats depend on, and very low frequencies, which elephants and whales use to communicate over long distances.

Touch brings in a group of specialist nerve cells in the skin, to detect objects we come in contact with. We can tell whether these objects are hot or cold, hard or soft, sharp or flat, painful or pleasurable, liquid or dry, so it's clearly not a single sense.

Taste is a chemical sense, activating receptor cells on our tongues. It's quite limited in the information it can provide, and probably evolved to help us tell whether things are good to eat or are toxic. It works closely with our sense of smell. Hold your nose and you can't tell if you're eating an apple or an onion.

Smell is the major chemical sense in our bodies. We can recognise several hundred chemical molecules individually through a kind of lock and key mechanism on the receptor surface. The larger this receptor surface, the more molecules can be recognised. Other animals, such as dogs, can recognise several thousand molecules. The receptors can respond to different molecular shapes, indeed a whole class of organic compounds are classed as 'aromatics', because of our ability to smell those which contain a six-carbon ring. (And they don't all smell nice). We respond too to organic molecules containing nitrogen, sulphur and oxygen. Highly reactive molecules are likely to be toxic, so that's probably why this system evolved, and so powerfully. We run away from the smell of smoke, from volcanic fumes, from the smells of decay and death; and we're attracted to kitchens, for the smells of cooking. Pheromones are chemicals which we can detect without being aware of them. They're used for communication of status between individuals in the same species, and they produce behavioural responses such as desire or fear. Some animals have a vomero-nasal organ which is used to detect, say, whether a potential mate is in season or not. You may see them sniff, then raise their heads and roll their upper lips back. Ethologists call this the Flehmen response.

> sight of falling leaves
> scent of damp October day
> cry of a heron
> an evening meal with good wine
> that ends with a warm handshake

Of course these senses aren't the only ones. What about our sense of balance? That comes from structures in our inner ears. Is there a sense of time? Assuredly. Even plants sense the difference between day and night, when to make flowers, when to drop their leaves. A sense of direction? Some birds migrate, and that would be impossible without some kind of GPS. Speed? Well, we can certainly detect acceleration. And some fish can detect electrical activity generated by their prey. That makes ten senses, and I'm sure there are more. So why do we talk about five senses? It doesn't make sense.

Go fly a kite

Back in my childhood it was my brother Graeme who had an interest in kites, and other things you could build with your hands. I was phenomenally clumsy and cack-handed, verging on the dyspraxic. But I could get interested in the theoretical side of things, like the drawings of Cody kites, those precursors of powered aircraft, in the pages of the Eagle comic.

Flight was something I left to the birds, although I didn't see an eagle until much later, and didn't make my first flight in an aircraft until I was in my thirties. One, I think it was.

Every time I tried to fly someone else's kite it was a failure. I couldn't grasp the techniques needed to keep the things aloft, and nobody had written a book about the subject that I could read to master the theory. Flying kites was a frustrating business, and I usually gave up after a couple of nose dives.

On a Normandy beach I once watched a Frenchman (I presume) trying to launch one of those stunt kites; things of beauty which can loop the loop and sweep majestically through the skies, reaching improbable heights. His didn't. Time after time it would catch the wind, rise, do a couple of twirls, then accelerate into the sand. 'Flew like a tent peg,' as Biggles might have said. Time after time he would dig it out, wind up the string, or whatever the technical term is, and throw it into the air again. His wife (I presume again) sat on her towel, wearing her dark glasses, reading a book, smoking, not saying a word. This is a marriage, I remember thinking, that will not end well. Too many downs, not enough ups.

But I remember, in Tian 'An Men Square, seeing children's kites fluttering in the smog above. That might be fun, I thought. And back home, on Dunbar's Belhaven beach, power kites are flown whenever it's windy, which is most days. But not by me.

> up up and away
> holding onto the taut line
> as the wind catches

Section IV

How it nearly ended

Legs pulled from under me, and I don't know which way is up.
Mouth and nostrils fill with water, and I start to choke and drown.

It was a holiday to Oban, our first post-war family holiday. Private cars were few and far between in those days, and my father had bought an ex-military staff car, a soft-topped convertible, which he said was an Austin 8½, presumably because of its horse power. The roof leaked. I'm not complaining, just stating a fact, the roof leaked. We thought nothing of it. Didn't all cars leak?

We had a tent big enough for the four of us, made of heavy green canvas. My parents couldn't afford a hotel or a boarding house, and there were social reasons why they would not have liked staying in someone else's house. Camping was fine though, it was universal, everyone could camp. I wonder sometimes if the years my father spent living under canvas in the Egyptian desert during the war might have steered his inclinations towards camping? Impossible to say, but he enjoyed it. One of the things I remember about camping in those days is that if it was raining you couldn't touch the fabric above your head, or it would lose its waterproof qualities and let in water.

The first night it poured, and my father couldn't find a camp site—they were thin on the ground in those days—so we pitched the tent inside a wartime Nissen hut made of corrugated iron, without front or back, just by the roadside. It was at Brig O' Turk, in the Trossachs, a decent mileage for the first afternoon's driving. In the morning the rain had stopped, and my father drove back to the village to buy rolls for our breakfast. After that we hit the highway, although we wouldn't have called it that then. We reached our destination, the campsite at Ganavan Sands, just outside Oban, by late evening. At the head of each steep section of every Highland road was a car park, and here everyone stopped to lift the car bonnets to let the engines cool. Another thing my father always did on journeys was to cut the engine and coast down hills in neutral, to save petrol. This was fairly common too.

My father was a good oarsman, and one afternoon he hired a rowing boat and took us out to sea. I could see down to the depths of the very clear water, to the kelp beds waving in the swell, and the darkness of the deepest water, where heaven knows what monsters lurked.

So my little brother and I played on the beach, building sandcastles with our buckets and spades, cutting canals to channel the water—they always collapsed. Later I somehow drifted away from Graeme and my parents, drawn by the screams and laughter from the breaking waves, which were quite sizeable that day. I jumped over the foam and the waves, gradually getting deeper and deeper, until an incoming wave picked me up and tumbled me over and over, gasping and confused. I was terrified. There were people on either side of me, but they didn't seem to realise the danger I was in. I can recall seeing the underside of a breaking wave, one which somehow pushed me back to the shore. On hands and knees, coughing and spluttering, I stumbled from the sea.

What I cannot forget is the laughter of my fellow wave-jumpers. They thought it was funny, or maybe they just didn't appreciate that I was not waving, but drowning. That was where it ended for me; that blind trust in others, that feeling I could rely on other people to look after me. After that I knew I was on my own; it was up to me to look after myself. I learned how to swim.

> jumping over waves
> then the larger breakers come
> pulling me under

Poets and trees

What a difference a shaft of sunlight makes to these autumn trees. The mist and rain of yesterday departed, I'm looking out on a vista of greens, browns, russets and yellows stretching far down the North Esk River. The river banks open out near Musselburgh, but here they are steep and beautiful, dripping dead leaves and the remains of last night's rain. There was talk at breakfast of strong winds and heavy downpours last night but, to be honest, behind the thick walls of this Castle I noticed nothing.

There is something deeply comforting, I feel, in being among Big Trees. I didn't see the Giant Redwoods of California, but I walked through a grove of their reasonably giant cousins, the Coastal Redwoods, at Big Sur. They are immense and ancient, have lived here for centuries, and contact with human history made little impact until recently.

Two of the four gardens which make up the Royal Botanic Garden Edinburgh,where I worked for fifteen years, are particularly noted for their trees. The Younger Botanic Garden at Benmore, Argyll, is on a wooded hillside on Scotland's west coast. This is an area infamous for its high rainfall, so it's natural that it would have a good collection of North American West Coast conifers, and it does. Some of its trees are the largest examples of their species anywhere in Britain. There's a stunningly beautiful avenue of Giant Redwood, but they haven't yet attained their full height. Give them time. Sitka Spruce, Noble Fir, Hemlock, Western Red Cedar and Douglas Fir all grow well here, some of them champion trees.

In the colder, drier East of Scotland near Peebles, Dawyck Botanic Garden also has some wonderful trees, including the 'Dawyck Beech', although they are perhaps not quite as tall as those at Benmore. I recently went there to compose a renga, at the invitation of Gerry Loose, following a similar renga with Mandy Haggith at the Edinburgh garden. Both poets were ensconced in their respective gardens for the 'Walking With Poets'

project, sponsored by the Scottish Poetry Library and the Royal
Botanic Garden Edinburgh. Poets and trees go together well.

> table lamp switched off
> the tower now in sunlight
> golden trees below

Deaths in Spain

The Valle de los Caídos, Valley of the Fallen, was built by General
Franco over a 20 year period, to commemorate those killed on
both sides during the Spanish Civil War. It stands in the midst
of the majestic hard hills of the Sierra de Guadarrama.

I thought it was a mournful and desolate place, and I felt
uncomfortable being there, where the Generalissimo himself
is buried. It was carved deep into the mountain, out of the grey
granite, by prisoners of war, of whom an unknown number lost
their lives. A basilica was built, later blessed by Pope John XXIII,
and it's the resting place for 40,000 coffins. In the centre there's a
high, domed chamber, decorated with portraits of the distinguished
dead. The guide says Franco's face is here, but I couldn't make
it out. As soon as I look vertically upward at the inside of the
dome, with concentric circles of portraits above me, I find I can't
focus on individual faces. It is, literally, a dizzying experience.

Outside the monument, on top of the mountain, there's an
enormous crucifix. It may impress some people, but to me its
presence jars; it's a man-made intrusion into natural grandeur. It
stands to exonerate an evil dictator, and to atone for his many
many sins, but to me it dishonours the mountain.

Let the fallen stay fallen, let them be remembered in the words
of those who were there, and in the minds of those who read
their words and keep them in their hearts.

> a cavern of death
> in the high Spanish mountains
> it's raining up here

The Streets of Toledo

Our first view of Toledo is as El Greco might have seen it—a dark stormy morning, heavy rain turning the soil a deeper red, sky full of ragged sombre clouds. The Rio Tajo (which becomes the Tejo or Tagus whether it knows it or not) is green and silty, a bright chiffon scarf wound round three sides of the ancient ochre city. We feel a keen sense of anticipation as we step through the gates onto the cobbled streets: after all, we are new here, and we prefer to experience novelty rather than read guidebooks.

The vast cathedral is in the process of having its ceiling restored, requiring a forest of scaffolding and the incessant noise of hammering. No matter, we are awed, as its makers intended back in the 13th century. In the Sacristy we see saints illuminated by El Greco, Velasquez and Titian, and in the Chapter House serried ranks of cardinals fill the walls. El Greco's masterpiece—*The Burial of the Count of Orgaz*—is in a little church nearby. It is an allegory for the ascent of the soul of a good man into heaven, attended by saints. The soul itself is portrayed as a featureless and faceless baby, about to enter an inverted birth canal composed of cloud, and leading to Heaven. It's a disturbing image, reminding us how much our mental pictures of the world have changed over the centuries. We've become used to seeing Renaissance masterpieces cleaned and restored, with brilliant reds and blues replacing the brown patina of ancient varnish, but El Greco's colours here are muted and subtle. In particular his blues are dark, and shadowed with black.

The rain has stopped when we emerge, blinking, into the light. The old synagogue, built by Moorish craftsmen for the Sephardic community in the 12th century, is a reminder that Christians, Muslims and Jews mostly shared this city in harmony until 1492, when the Jews were forced to convert or leave Spain. Near here a few years ago King Juan Carlos tore up a copy of the infamous decree, in the presence of Arabic and Israeli Heads of State, but there are still no Jews in Toledo. Until this visit I had not known that the Year of Discovery was also a Year of Intolerance.

as the river moves
between Spain and Portugal
a sudden name change

Hero City

It was still Leningrad back in 1982. There was still a Soviet Union, and Leonid Brezhnev was its Prime Minister. The Soviet Union consisted of fifteen Autonomous Republics, which were nothing of the kind, and our Intourist 'minder' made us memorize them on a later bus trip to the Caucasus. I still think of it as Leningrad, can't get used to St Petersburg. I remember the bright summer sun glinting off the gilded spire of the Peter and Paul Fortress, and the golden statues in the Peterhof after a hydrofoil trip from the embankment. I remember the fountains, including the trick ones which soak the unwary, and the grounds which reminded me of Versailles, but in a good way. I remember Revolution Square and the Field of Mars. I'll never forget the Winter Palace—The Hermitage—its gates still looking as they did in Eisenstein's iconic film of the Revolution, the Mirrored Staircase, the Malachite Room, the Impressionists and Post-Impressionists, the *babushki* sitting in each room glaring at visitors. Equally unforgettable was our night at the ballet in the Mariinsky Theatre, the Kirov dancers performing Carmen, the Vietnamese tourist having a heart attack in the balcony during the third act. I remember the battleship 'Avrora' moored outside our hotel; whose salvo had signalled the start of the October Revolution in 1917. I remember walking along Nevsky Prospekt, and buying posters in Dom Knigi, truly a House of Books.

Most hauntingly, I recall the Museum of the Siege during the Great Patriotic War (that's what they call World War II), and the adjacent Piskarevskoye Cemetery, with its solemn music, eternal flame, and the mass graves where, we were told, half a million lie buried, most dying of starvation when German troops besieged the city between 1941 and 1944. The total death toll was probably around one million. The events of this time meant a lot to 'Leningrad'—Stalin named it 'Hero City'—but I'm not sure if they have the same resonance to 'St Petersburg'. And sometimes, when I think about our time there, I listen to Dmitri Shostakovich's 'Leningrad' symphony, the Seventh. Heroic music for heroic times, if you still believe in heroes.

drums for guns
and driving rhythms play
the march of history

Not leaving here

On the road to Ypres we detour to visit Tyne Cot cemetery, our
introduction to the scale of death in the Somme area. We visit the
Menin Gate, but I can't find the panel listing the Gordon Highlanders'
fallen. I presume most of any possible Buchan relatives would
have enlisted in that regiment. In any case, my interest at this stage
is an abstract one—none of mine died here, I think I know.

We settle into our billet at Hardecourt aux Bois, a converted
farm steading often rented out to battlefield tourists. One of
the outbuildings has been converted into a drinking den,
The Rum Ration, where we would have some memorable
sing-songs in the evenings ahead.

The following morning four of us walk up the road and cut
along the edge of a field, among Yellow Archangels, ground
ivy and wild hops. We emerge near the crossroads, where an
impressive shrine to a local World War I hero stands. Just across
from it I spot a fresh drainage ditch dug in the chalky subsoil.
I walk along it and find a deep, dark hole in the ground, with a
piece of corrugated iron roofing it. An artificial poppy has been
placed beside it. It is too dark to see inside, but it is obviously
an old trench, and one not marked on our trench map.

> a line of horsemen
> troop over the blasted ground
> n the old photo

We drive to the Thiepval Memorial, a massive monument designed
by Lutyens to commemorate the missing—those whose bodies had
never been identified. Flicking through the Register I find two who
share my surname, one indeed having the same name as my eldest
son. The shock has me gasping for breath and gulping back sobs.
Both lads were 19, and from Buchan, so they were almost certainly
related in some way to my family. We have brought with us a box
of crosses, each with a poppy, and I lay mine here to the memory

of David Will. In the visitor centre I check the database of Gordon Highlanders and discover another eleven Will names; more possible connections I hadn't known about. In Y Ravine cemetery I find a Mutch, my grandmother's maiden name, so there must be more.

Next morning a group of us revisit the trench I'd discovered. We find two bullets, a belt buckle, and some fragments of human bone—a rib and the head of a femur, smooth and unblemished by age or infirmity. 'They shall not grow old as we grow old' comes into my head. I'm just setting down the facts here, because it's difficult to convey the complexity and intensity of my emotions.

In the Serre No. 2 cemetery I find two more Will names; one from the London Scottish regiment, the other from a Canadian regiment. He had emigrated to Canada from Inverbervie and returned to Europe, only to die here. That has me in tears again. The German cemetery in Fricourt holds two large mass graves and many lines of iron crosses, among which we find the name of my German daughter-in-law's family, and Jane lays her cross here, although we do not know if there is any relationship. Our son lives and works in Germany, and I have two German grandchildren. Today our countries are close allies and friends, and I know that war between our nations is unthinkable, but that night in The Rum Ration the singing of 'A Gordon for me' sends a shiver down my spine, as the memory still does today.

Thanks to the Commonwealth War Graves Commission I now have the names and details of 25 relations for who the fields of Flanders were their last resting places.

> grassy fields, strange crops
> chalky soil and white gravestones
> sound of larks above

Only Connect

Down the road to the very nice coffee house and restaurant in Lasswade, *The Paper Mill*. It was once, you'll not be surprised to learn, a paper mill, on the banks of the North Esk River, before conversion. To the Fellows of Hawthornden its main attraction is that it offers, not just wi-fi, but free wi-fi, as the Castle has no internet connection. Last week all five of us bold Fellows piled into my car and drove down to check our emails and, yes, to have some coffee.

It must have been an amusing sight, five of us with our laptops open on a single table, hardly any room for the lattes. If we go there in the morning the very pleasant waiter always asks hopefully if we want to see the breakfast menu, but no, we really just want access to his bandwidth.

These days most writers are heavy users of the internet for research, for access to our websites, blogs, email, Skype facilities and social networking sites. So when we're here for four weeks we miss it.

And I especially miss seeing Jane. As I said to a fellow writer this morning, this is the longest period we've ever been apart in the 50 years of our relationship. And while I know I can nip home on Saturdays for a few hours, we really are both finding it difficult to cope with an enforced separation. Even if we do different things while we're at home, at least we manage to find time each day to talk. And we do talk a lot, sometimes over coffee.

> a coffee morning
> but not like any other
> I've experienced

Choices

Coming up for retirement we had been looking for a place by the sea to move to, a place with more to interest and stimulate us than the place we lived in. The East Neuk of Fife is somewhere we both love, and I know the coast particularly well, having walked the length of the coastal path: Lower Largo to Elie, St Monans, Pittenweem, Anstruther, Crail and Fife Ness. One of those towns would probably have been our first choice, but I was still working in Edinburgh, so Fife would have been impractical.

We looked at towns on the south side of the Forth (it had to be a reasonably sized town for the services, and with good transport connections to Edinburgh), but none of them had the combination of features we sought. We both enjoyed visiting North Berwick, had done since our childhoods and those of our children, but property prices were higher than we could afford.

Then one Sunday morning you said you hadn't been to Dunbar in more than twenty years, and should we have a look at it? My last trip to Dunbar was probably even further back in time, and my memories even vaguer, but we set off. Forgetting what the town looked like, when we reached West Barns and saw the Car Park sign we thought the main town would be just a short walk. We discovered our mistake and drove on to Dunbar High Street. In a sunny late summer day we walked down to the harbour and saw a seal swimming between the fishing boats. We turned to each other and said, 'This is the place,' and it was. Three months later we had sold up and moved in.

I was still working, had nearly three years to go before retirement, so I joined the commuters on the platform at Dunbar station every morning. (I did remember the station and its colourful little garden). I left my bicycle in Waverley station overnight, so when I arrived I would jump on the bike and pedal downhill to *The Botanics*. Each evening I pedalled back up the hill and padlocked the bike.

We made the right choice.

hermit crab
tries on different shells
finds the one that fits

Bag End Sur Mer

We moved to Dunbar at the end of November, 2000. It was only after we had moved in that we realised our new home was smaller than our old one. It had one more room than our old house had, and it was all on one level, but the rooms were smaller than we had anticipated. We were taken in by the charm and the décor, and we had viewed it in the evening, without our measuring tape. We hadn't even noticed that the East Coast Main Line was only fifty yards away from our front door! It had less room for our belongings—our dining area furniture and my book collection in particular. I had floored the loft in my old place, and I realised I'd very quickly have to do the same here. Our new garage was piled high with books in cardboard boxes, and so was my little 'study'. Working evenings and weekends, I was finally able to move some books upstairs, squeeze over boxes into my room, set up the computer, and start writing again.

I was still working at the time, and I had begun to commute into Edinburgh. Coming home, I would step off the train in the winter darkness, inhale the smell of the sea, and walk home along Queens Road. When the tide was in and the swell was up I could see the ghostly white waves sweeping in below me, and hear the sound of them breaking on the unseen beach. Some nights the moon was up, and I could see its silver light, a searchlight on the sea. The lighthouse at Barns Ness was still operating then, and its beam swept out regularly. I counted the double flashes of light from the Isle of May lighthouse. The train journey was also a novelty. In Mid Calder I had driven to and from work, and, although I hadn't realised it, that must have been a stress. On the train I could relax for the half hour or so it took to reach Dunbar.

Coming in to the house, the smell of the evening meal met me, warm and welcoming. We dined by candlelight in those early days, on either side of our heavy oak table, and these romantic winter evenings were a magical introduction to our new lives by the sea. We started to unwind, to slow down, to explore the area, and I knew that when it came time for me to stop working too, our lives would be enriched by our move.

winter soups and stews
eaten by flickering light
room to start breathing

Killing time

The train journey from Dunbar to Edinburgh and vice versa,
is scheduled to take around 25 minutes. Most days it does, give
or take a few minutes. I remember one time it didn't, when a
man stepped in front of the train on a level crossing. Heartless,
I think, to make a train driver, an innocent person undeserving
of the inevitable distress and guilt which will follow, be the agent
of your demise, when you no longer wish to go on living.

Most days, if I had a window seat, I would spend the journey time
looking out at the fields and farms, the woods and villages, the
distant Forth, as the train hurtled along at 100 m.p.h. One early
summer morning I saw an otter jinking along a path beside a
small stream, a tributary of the River Tyne. That's not Newcastle's
Tyne, but the one which flows through East Lothian, meeting the
sea near Dunbar. I was so pleased to see the otter, shy and rarely
observed in the South of Scotland, even if the sighting was brief.

If the weather was poor, or if I didn't have a seat by the window,
I would sometimes work on the novel I had started writing
the previous year. With a hardcover notebook I could write
a couple of pages of my story, albeit in very shaky handwriting,
before the train arrived in the station.

Most journeys I sat amongst strangers in the crowded carriage,
but sometimes I had friends to talk to. If not, there was always the
notebook. One day I was writing a section set on a Mediterranean
beach in the South of France. My characters were enjoying a swim
and a picnic. I was interrupted by a child throwing a tantrum, a few
seats behind me. Every time I thought the scene was over it would
start up again. It was, to say the least, distracting. Eventually, out of
frustration, I did the unthinkable. Gentle Reader, I killed a character
in my story, without qualm or remorse. I had him drown in the Med.
It didn't stop the child crying, but it gave me a feeling of satisfaction.

> otter by the burn
> as the moving train speeds by
> green wheat growing tall

Jazz ways

I discovered jazz as a teenager, acquired a second-hand clarinet, then a second-hand alto sax, started playing by ear, apart from an interesting excursion into Handel with the school orchestra, which was not a total success. I listened to jazz on the radio, and went to concerts in Edinburgh. I remember seeing the John Dankworth Orchestra, with Dudley Moore on piano, the Modern Jazz Quartet, Sonny Stitt, Ronnie Ross and Ronnie Scott. I met Tubby Hayes at an Art Club dance, and discussed Ornette Coleman with him and Alan Bold—another Scottish poet who also played alto at that time.

I used to go to jazz clubs in Edinburgh, jamming if I was allowed, but it was awkward, since I lived in Bathgate and didn't have a car. The last bus left Edinburgh at 10:30, so I often had to sleep rough, or walk the streets carrying my sax case, until the first morning bus home. I played in a small local band—*The Vikings*—for dances and socials, but that wasn't really jazz, not really what I wanted to play. I was so much the musician that when I left home to work a ten-week gig as a barman in the English Lake District, I really missed my instruments. I asked my father to put the music case on a bus for Keswick, and it was delivered the next day. You could do that then, long before the days of Fedex or UPS. At least now I could play in break times, down by Lake Bassenthwaite, if it wasn't raining.

The trouble was that I couldn't really decide if I wanted to be a writer or a musician, and then I met Jim Haynes, owner of The Paperback book shop in Charles Street. It was then the first and only UK bookshop specialising in paperback books, and he stocked material impossible to buy anywhere else—*Evergreen Review*, Ian Hamilton Finlay's broadsheet *Poor. Old. Tired. Horse.* I bought Donald Allen's anthology *New American Poetry, 1945–1960* (I still have it), and music began to take second place. I came down on the side of becoming a writer, and I seem to have succeeded, but it took me a long time.

There was the small matter of earning a steady income; there was falling in love and getting married; there was starting a family and building a career, and that career turned out to be quite successful. In short, I stopped writing for more than 20 years, didn't even miss it because I was so busy. I began writing again in the 1980s, started to get published, and I've never looked back. The break from jazz was even longer; my instruments staying in the loft for 30 years. But my favourite listening was and still is tenor jazz. I always thought I should have been a tenor player, so now I've bought myself a tenor sax, and I'm learning to play it properly, this time through reading music and learning musical theory, not just playing by ear. And when I play it's like I'm falling in love all over again. I still write a bit too.

> memorised the solos
> on Kind of Blue
> getting my chops back

MJQ

One of the first jazz concerts I went to was when I was still
at school. The Modern Jazz Quartet were billed to appear
at Edinburgh's Usher Hall, and I went along, excited to hear
a live performance from a band I'd only heard on radio—I
didn't have a record player then. This was their only Scottish
appearance on their UK tour. Must have been 1959, I think.

They came on stage, dressed very formally in tuxedos and black
bow ties. Their leader, the pianist John Lewis, was then exploring
links between jazz and classical music, so the formality was
important to them—they wanted to be taken seriously.

And when they started playing, they were. The audience, myself
included, listened with rapt attention. At that time Lewis had just
finished scoring the Roger Vadim film, *No Sun in Venice*, and
part of their set was the music from the film. One of my favourite
pieces, then and now, was *The Golden Striker*. Lewis's delicate piano
was complemented by Milt Jackson's lyrical vibraphone playing,
Connie Kay's subtle cymbal work, and the sonorous bowed bass
of Percy Heath. I was enthralled, and it encouraged me to listen
to more adventurous and complex music than I'd heard before.

I discovered later that Milt Jackson, a shy self-effacing man with a
phenomenal talent, and a lightness of touch which took my breath
away, was a big fan of boxing, watching televised fights when he
wasn't on stage. You'd never have known it from his demeanour
or his free-flowing improvisations, but that's people, isn't it?

> four suits on the stage
> formal, black and dignified
> swinging, in control

An ending

I was born in July 1942. My father was by then in Egypt, serving in the Royal Air Force, building and repairing aircraft instruments. He must have come home on leave in late October 1943, because my brother was born the following August. At the end of the war he was not demobilised immediately; his skills were in demand in an aircraft factory in Dumbarton. It wasn't until 1946 that he finally returned home, to two wee bairns who didn't know him. Perhaps this was the reason he and I failed to bond, then or later.

Sadly, I never really felt close to him. It was as if we lived in different worlds, spoke different languages. To me, my brother Graeme, and to my mother, he could be a bully. Sometimes he would lash out in anger and frustration. And yet he was totally different with my youngest brother Stephen, born when I was 13. When my two children were born he was very fond of them, and they of him. In company he was well liked, very popular, jovial, a man with many friends and some secrets.

Several times over the years he fell out with me, would refuse to talk to me. Our final argument was just a couple of years before his death, after which we never spoke again. He forbade my mother to phone me from their home in Perthshire. Sometimes, if she knew he would be out playing golf for some time, she would make surreptitious phone calls to keep me in touch.

And then came 9/11. My mother told me he had watched the television footage of the attacks on the Twin Towers and their collapse with increasing agitation and high emotion. He could not stop watching the newsreels. Two days later she phoned me at work to say he'd had a massive stroke. By the time I reached Perth Royal Infirmary he was dead.

The hospital staff were very considerate; they took me to a room for a last viewing of his body and stood aside as I paid my respects. I touched his cold face, his cold hand, stepped back, bowed, and said goodbye.

difficult to say
but that's the way
it was

Family photo

These days, the family only gets together for funerals, but this one was taken at a wedding, maybe in the late fifties or very early sixties. It's black-and-white, not posed, but the image is crisp and well-defined. It's outside a Register Office in central Edinburgh. My parents are there, off to the side, behind some iron railings, my father open-mouthed, obviously laughing at something. He was always eager, easily moved to laughter or rage. My mother is smiling too, well-dressed in the fashion of the day. When or if I compose my history, how will I account for the division of genes that made me? When I was small I sometimes thought I was adopted, but the physical features and susceptibilities I now exhibit clearly come from both of them.

My paternal grandmother is in the picture. I never met my mother's mother—she was dead before I was born. Granny stayed with us in Bathgate when she was getting on in years, and I remember seeing increasing signs of Alzheimer's, although I didn't know that's what it was. She died in a nursing home in Edinburgh, now converted into flats. That was the subject of another photograph: father, mother, granny, Jane, my brother Stephen, late brother Graeme, outside on the steps. Funny how many photographs are taken on steps. Not funny really, it makes sense; you can get more people into a photo if they're standing at different levels.

Anyway, back to the wedding group. The Aunts are mostly there. My mother had six sisters, most of them formidable women. Rena's man Johnnie is there, a nice man, but desperately hen-pecked. I can't see Rena, but she was very short, possibly hidden in the crush. Ina was very short too, but I don't think she was at the wedding. Isa was taller, and she had the same fashion-consciousness as my mother. Both were expert seamstresses, maybe taking that from their father, who was a drunken ne'er-do-well tailor. The sisters ganged up on him and threw him out of the house when he drank the housekeeping for the final time.

Uncle Jim and Aunt Alice are there—she's wearing a big picture hat and a toothy grin. Alice came from Morpeth and I liked her a lot. Jim was mum's elder brother. Her younger brother David is here with his lover Tom. They were a nice couple. David died of a complication on the operating table—supposed to be minor elective surgery, but it killed him. Tom was inconsolable at the funeral, and Jim did the oration.

The groom, my cousin Alistair, is dressed in a formal tail suit, which doesn't suit him—he wasn't like that—but his father, my Uncle James, was a very formal person. Joyce was the bride, a nice cheery friendly woman. Remind me to tell you their story some time, when you come again. More tea?

> face the camera
> come closer in at the sides
> here's your history

Death in the family

My father had three sons—me, Graeme, 2 years younger, and Stephen, 13 years after me. His elder brother James also had three sons—Stewart, Douglas and Alistair. They lived in a cottage in Aberlady, by the sea. Aunt Meg used to swim in the sea every day, summer or winter, rain or shine. I remember trips from the city down to see them; the boys were older than me, and a bit boisterous. One time they put me in a cart and wheeled me along the street at speed, until I fell out and cut my head. My mother was hopeless where blood was concerned, so it was Aunt Meg who cut my bloody hair off and cleaned the wound, putting a lump of butter on the swelling—you did that in those days.

Anyway, they grew up, as we did. Stewart became a policeman, moved south, and joined the Met, rising to the rank of Sergeant. Alistair met Joyce, a Highland lass, and they moved to Dunbar. Douglas became a chemist, worked for BP at the Grangemouth petrochemical place. Every year the three brothers, with their families, would arrange their holidays so they could spend some time together by the sea at North Berwick. Sometimes our family would join them, but more often not. And then one year, with an onshore breeze piling up the waves, a teenage girl got into difficulties in the surf. A young student went into the water to help her, and then he too started to struggle. So Stewart, a strong swimmer, went into the water. The upshot was that Stewart and the student drowned, and the girl managed to scramble to safety.

That was the end of the annual seaside get-togethers. A year later, Alistair and Joyce, with their teenage twins, were driving north to visit her mother. Coming up behind an illegally overloaded log carrier, Stewart did not see the logs which fell off and came through the windscreen, killing him, Joyce, and their 15-year old daughter. Their son Gavin was injured but survived, damaged severely by what had happened.

So that led to a triple funeral in Dunbar Parish Church which I will never forget. Twenty years later, when we moved to Dunbar, people still fondly remembered the family. Meg, shattered by the loss in quick succession of two sons, a daughter-in-law and a granddaughter, didn't live much longer. I remember seeing her shaking her head during the funeral, when the minister talked about them being in a better place. Gavin went to live with his grandfather in the family home in Dunbar, but it wasn't a happy situation. He moved away and now lives in a town in England.

My brother Graeme died of cancer in 1991, aged 47. Douglas is still in Grangemouth with his family. I moved to Dunbar in 2000. I think about the two brothers and their six sons. I think about the sea, and the excitement of storms. And to this day I'm very wary of log carriers on the road.

> living by the sea
> summer fun and sudden death
> the power of waves

Paint your picture, Sir?

Wherever tourists go, you'll find artists offering to paint their portraits, either a lightning sketch or a measured sitting. The little square at the top of Montmartre is thronged with them and their easels, examples of previous work, and little stools for the punter to sit on while the portrait is completed. Artists not currently occupied are always on the lookout for new commissions, mostly in a good-natured way, but I've never been tempted to take them up on their offers. In Beijing, outside the quarters of the Dowager Empress Cixi, the power behind the throne, an artist offered to paint my portrait on a dinner plate. He was very persistent, making sketches, painting and overpainting them, but I ignored him. He tried again. I said 'No Thanks' in English, but that had no effect. Eventually I tried my sketchy Chinese—'*bu, xiexie ni*'—very politely (as you can tell), but he ignored this too. Maybe my inflexion was wrong. Finally I stood up and walked away, to look at the room where new Imperial concubines were brought to the Emperor, gift-wrapped and hidden inside silk rugs. The painter washed the blue paint from his plate with water from a water bottle, and went off in search of a new target.

My granddaughter once drew my portrait with crayons, and sent it to me as a birthday card. I framed it, old softie that I am. A friend once drew a cartoon portrait of me. I thought it made me look like an old male orang-utan, but maybe that's what he intended.

You once painted my portrait, and it captures my likeness very well, but I can't look at it: it makes me feel uncomfortable. I'm wearing a black leather jacket and my favourite black fedora, and looking ever so definitely pretentious. Your painting, done in acrylics, treats the skin tones very impressionistically, with splashes of vivid colours that look natural when viewed from a distance, only I can't view it from any distance. I think it's the eyes that unnerve me: I don't want to look into them.

Of course I've had my photograph taken many times, the earliest one nude, on the beach at Aberdour, at one year old, and posted to 'My darling Daddy' in Egypt, 1943. Friends and family have photographed me on holiday, in pubs and restaurants, at poetry readings and elsewhere. And being an author, I'm often asked to supply publicity photos for events, festivals, book jackets, websites and the like. I prefer to use photos taken by professionals for these purposes, but they have to be reasonably up to date. I've seen some author photos taken 20 or more years previous, and under very flattering conditions, that I've put on websites for them. Maybe I really should be honest, tell them that they constitute breaches of the Trade Descriptions Act? The camera often lies, but your audience will find you out.

> look in the mirror
> see the face of a stranger
> before you were you

You're crowding me

How many sayings are there about crowds? Two's company ... Too many cooks ..., A crowd is not company (Bacon), The madding crowd's ignoble strife (Gray), In marriage, three is company, and two none (Wilde, of course). Me, I'm uncomfortable in crowds. I've never been to a football match, unless you count the one when our 11-year old son's team lost 22 nil, so he never played again. I've never been to a pop concert, in an arena or anywhere else crowd psychology or mass hysteria could arise. I've been to jazz concerts, but that's different; they're usually in halls or theatres, and the audience members are individuals coolly listening, just groovin on our own, man, never a crowd.

Frankly the thought of crowds scares me; their unpredictability, potential for chaos, possibility of physical danger are all things I try to avoid. I remember going to a Hogmanay celebration in Edinburgh one year. It was before the event really took off, went international then global, but there were a quarter of a million people in Princes Street and on the Mound, with no crowd control except some overworked police. The press of people became truly frightening. And, let me be frank and hope no Gentle Reader will be offended, the streets were awash with urine, casually dispensed, as no portaloos were provided.

We'd met our son (not the ex-footballer, the other one) and his girlfriend, and taken them to a Thai restaurant, not knowing he didn't like Thai food. You and I did though. Then we walked for ages and joined the throng in Princes Street. The fireworks were terrific, and the classical music wafting up from the orchestra in the Gardens was inaudible. Rather rashly I was wearing the kilt, and I lost count of the number of young women, having taken drink, who lifted my kilt to see if I was a 'true Scotsman'. Was I? As the saying goes, a lady never asks, and a gentleman never tells. Still, the Castle Rock was a magnificent backdrop for the show, we had a great time, and we vowed we'd never go again.

no space between us
waves of movement spread throughout
winter festival

Weighty matters

Back in February I was working on my allotment. The plots are about a mile outside Dunbar, and overlooked only by an agricultural machinery yard, so it's remote and isolated. On this particular day there was no-one else around. I was planting my onion sets, as you do, bending over with the dibber to make the holes, and dropping the small bulbs into them.

I became aware that my vision was blurring, and that I was becoming dizzy and disoriented. I managed to stagger over to my shed, and leaned against it until things went back to normal. Rather stupidly, I then went back to what I'd been doing, and exactly the same thing happened again.

So I thought I'd better see my GP. He examined me, and said that it was probably the result of being overweight, with the excess being primarily round my waist. When I bent over I was compressing the major blood vessel in my abdomen, the *vena cava*, and preventing the blood from reaching my brain. He advised me to lose weight.

That's been my motivation. I started immediately, cutting my portions in half, and avoiding carbohydrates. A slice of bread or a couple of potatoes became very desirable but occasional luxuries. Lunch was most often miso soup, often with some vegetables. I increased my intake of fruit and veg, and reduced my caffeine intake. I have two cups of coffee a day now, which is way fewer than I used to drink. At the same time I increased my exercise regime. I've been going to the gym regularly for many years, but now I concentrated on aerobic exercise—treadmill, cross-trainer, bike and rowing machines. I started running on the treadmill, gradually building up speed and duration. I'm now very comfortable with the regime of diet and exercise.

Gradually, and without putting pressure on myself, I've gone from 14 stone to just under 12. I've kept it steady, losing about 2 lbs per week, but I don't beat myself up if I don't achieve that, and the effects have been dramatic.

I feel better than I have in years; I don't get breathless digging or bending down to tie my shoelaces. I've got so much more energy. On the BMI scale I've gone from obese through overweight to 'normal weight'. I can get into clothes I haven't worn for years. The only downside is that the Sheila Flett ring Jane gave me when we visited Orkney no longer fits my finger—I can't wear it. And the wedding ring that gave me such problems in Lithuania has had to be taken down two sizes after it dropped off my finger at the allotment. I was lucky to find it.

Will I lose more weight? Well, maybe a little. I don't have a target weight, but a target shape. There's still a bulge round the waist, albeit it's a much smaller one. The onions were lovely.

> falling down worry
> diet, exercise, lose weight
> keeps the heart beating

New Road Layout Ahead

We move to a housing estate just being built, one of the first 12 houses in a development of over 100 homes, including a new school for the village. It needs access roads to link it to the centre of the village, and to the road network of the rapidly expanding New Town of Livingston. So connections are made, and a country lane becomes the main road to the village and beyond. A T-junction is put in, and the road signs go up.

Some drivers, coming off the busy A71, drive at excessive speeds, ignoring the speed limit signs Before new houses were built in the field over the fence from us, we had a clear view of the junction. I miss the horses that grazed in that field—it filled up with houses before we moved.

So it is that one Saturday morning, working in our back garden, we see a car take the junction far too fast. It swerves and wobbles, before flipping over sideways and somersaulting a couple of times, coming to rest the right way up. But we had seen, as it spun through the air, a large object detach itself from the vehicle, fly up and land on the pavement. We thought it was a body thrown clear by the violence of the accident, so we run towards it.

The driver is standing by his wrecked car, shaken but unhurt. What we had seen was his engine, torn free from its mounting and hurled into the air.

> speed kills, says the sign
> speed frightens the onlookers
> the horses graze on

Moonlight walks

Back in my spotty youth I was in the Boy Scouts for a couple of years. I've no recollection of why I joined—not for the uniform. I still don't know the function of the woggle. Some weekends we'd go camping to a place the Scouts had at Bonaly, in the Pentland foothills. One night our Assistant Scoutmaster thought to give us a challenge by organising a night-time walk in the countryside. We stumbled along, tripped on unseen obstacles, but we reached our objective and got back safely.

These days night vision goggles and other accessories are state of the art, with photomultiplier chips amplifying light so it's almost as clear as daylight. Modern armies usually prefer to attack at night, judging that their enemies won't be as well equipped as they are. They're usually right. And what would wildlife photography be without infrared cameras and the more advanced starcams? Infrared's quite simple really. You use an infra-red beam instead of a light beam to illuminate your target, and capture the images with a camera sensitive to infra-red frequencies—like light waves but longer. The animals you're filming can't see your beam, although the smaller ones may feel a touch warmer (IR is close to heat in the electromagnetic spectrum). Starcams are photomultipliers, amplifying meagre illumination from a few photons many times until the view is nearly as good as in daylight.

I liked walking in Calder Wood Country Park when we lived in Mid Calder—it's why I called my publishing business Calder Wood Press. We, and the children, had many happy days in the woods, in all seasons. One summer night, no doubt remembering my scouting days, I suggested to the boys, by then teenagers, that we go for a moonlight walk in the woods. Once our eyes were used to it, we could see fairly clearly by the moon's light, and in any case we were very familiar with the paths which criss-cross the wood. Over at the far side, in the disused shale mine tunnels, a group of local youngsters used to hang out, take drugs, and generally Get Up To No Good. We were about halfway across the park when they became aware of us, goodness how, and started chasing us. If you haven't tried it yourself, it's quite difficult to run through a wood at night, pursued by footpads or worse. We could hear them shouting behind us, so we kept running, down the track, over the Murieston Water, and up the hill to the street lights, hearts pounding. I've never written about this until now.

running in the dark
too late to eat more carrots
fears of the hunted

To the village

I make my mother her breakfast porridge, chat to the carer who is
giving her the morning combination of medicines, then set off to the
village to do some light shopping—the morning paper, some fruit,
detergent. The houses are arranged in a circular grand design, with
cul-de-sacs forming short spurs off an inner circle. In the centre is
a large grassy area with a few trees, almost randomly planted. No
ball games are permitted here, as the overwhelming majority of the
residents are elderly. The gardens are generally full of flowers, except
for a few houses whose owners have covered theirs with gravel chips.
That's an admission of defeat, I think, for it's not too difficult to
maintain a colourful garden.

The rain, which has caused severe flooding in regions south of the
hills within which the village nestles, is just beginning to fall here.
Dark spots appear on the pavement. At first they evaporate—this is,
after all, summer—then they become more numerous and begin to
merge. Raindrops splash on the puddles at the kerbside.

Coming to the grass circle, I strike out in a straight line, across the
diameter, as my route to the village begins in the lane off the cul-de-
sac directly opposite my mother's street. If this was a route commonly
used, no doubt there would by now be a trodden path, something
the landscapers call a 'desire line', but it seems I'm in a minority here.
The only others I've seen here have been dog walkers, allowing their
pets to sniff the grass at the end of elastic leads, clutching or hiding
polythene bags for the inevitable messes.

Nearing the children's play area the rain begins to get heavier, and
my phone rings, announcing the arrival of a text message. I pause to
reply. The rain is not unpleasant, I am wearing my waterproof jacket
and a hat. Summer rain doesn't force you to take cover, as winter
rain does.

On the return walk I pass a teenage girl with a cheerful, open, smiling
face. When you're young, life is an internal business; later you are

caught up in the delirious business of living, with no thought for the inevitable ending of things. Me? I've lived so long that I don't fear death. What I fear is dying.

a doggy area
so I keep my eyes down
on the wet grass

Barney's trip

Barney was unsettled. Tied by a leash to a rail in the lounge he walked
one way then the other as the leash shortened and tangled round
his neck. The rest of us were calm yet excited at our project about
to start, at the school in Benbecula, the wood at Langais, and the
art centre at Lochmaddy. For now we watched shearwaters flapping
and dipping over the wake's foamy thrust. Passing between the Inner
Hebrides islands as we did, we could judge their closeness by the
sight of seabirds flying out of their nests to fish. Gulls of various
kinds, gannets, and the auk family—puffins, tysties, razorbills, those
fast flutterers.

Alec took Barney for walks round the ship, but he felt, more directly
than we did, the shudder and throb of the ship's engines, transmitted
through the hull's steel plates, and it confused him. The concept of
a sea voyage doesn't make sense to dogs. Car journeys they can get
used to. They concentrate on what they can see and experience within
the car, but the movement of objects and places outside the windows
can upset them. What they know is what's beneath their feet and
under their noses. On this trip, the whiff of diesel exhaust, the smell
of the sea, cooking from the galley, and the odour of many strange
humans, including me, presented him with so many new sensations
that it was hard for him to understand this metal world moving on
top of the water.

I became very fond of him, that sweet, gentle dog, and in the days to
come I would take him for walks round the little island of Bailesheare
and over the causeway to the main island of North Uist. He got used
to me and I, never a dog owner, enjoyed these walks with him. I
talked to him, not feeling odd or self-conscious. He was a being I
could share discoveries with: the peewit swooping and circling over
the machair, the marsh marigold brightening the ditch at the side of
the road, the light on the sea and the white shell sand of the beach.

> wake spreads on both sides
> behind, a line of churned sea
> look out, look back, move

New shoes

You are wearing new shoes, which rub against some part of your foot which sticks up or sticks out or whatever—say the top of the instep - until you have a blister. So you put the new shoes aside for a couple of days and go back to the old ones until the blister heals. Then you put your new shoes on again, and it still hurts a bit, so you don't keep them on too long. You switch shoes back and forth over the next few days, until one day you realise your new shoes now fit you perfectly, that they're extremely comfortable. In fact, they've turned into your old shoes.

It's the same with people. It doesn't take long for a new acquaintance to become a good friend that you seem to have known for years. Count up the closeness though; measure the contact minutes. A lot less than you think. And what do you do with your old friends? Shove them in the bottom of the wardrobe, unless they are too obviously unfit for use. You may come across them from time to time, think, 'Oh, I remember so-and-so,' smile, maybe put them on again for old times' sake, until their behaviour makes you recall why you changed them in the first place. At some stage, whether you're a long-term hoarder or a regular spring-cleaner, you throw some out.

How many friends do I have now? Real friends, that is, not business contacts, occasional sightings, cafe society, people I know and smile to, but don't classify as friends, 'net friends? With family, with lovers, here and now gone maybe, the relationships are closer and more intimate. And how would you define a friend anyway? A confidante, someone I'm comfortable with? A person I can be myself with, so I don't have to pretend, to lie, to make up stuff? In my case, someone I'm happy to share space and time with, say on a mountain walk, without feeling an urge to say anything—I like my silent moments? Someone with whom I share an interest, an activity, a passion? No, there is more, but I'm not sure what it is. Maybe it's just people I've been around a long time. Old shoes.

> long walk on cliff path
> views of rocks, sea, birds, flowers
> feet are killing me

Burrowing

One of my Linlithgow friends emails me to say he is going to give a visiting American author a guided tour of Linlithgow Palace, and would I like to join them? He's an expert on Linlithgow, a former Provost, and I've always wanted to know more about it, so I immediately say yes. We agree to meet at the gates of St Michael's Church.

The Palace, built in the 15th century, was home to several Scottish Kings, and Mary, Queen of Scots, was born here in 1542, the daughter of King James V of Scotland and Mary of Guise. James died six days later, after defeat at the Battle of Solway Moss. Mary, who had in earlier times been wooed by Henry VIII, feared for the safety of her young daughter, and sent her to France to be brought up. The Palace is very substantial, built around a central courtyard which houses a statue of the Royal Beasts of Scotland, a lion and a unicorn, showing very clearly the non-equine elements of its nature. The Great Hall has been floored, and is now used for events, including international fashion shows.

But we start in the churchyard. We are shown the cover of a mort-safe, where the newly dead were laid until the onset of putrefaction. This was in the days of the Resurrectionists, who would dig up the bodies of the newly deceased and sell them to Anatomists for dissection. The mort-safe, common in many Scottish graveyards, made sure that the corpses were unsuitable for theft and retail, and after a suitable interval they were re-interred in more conventional graves elsewhere in the cemetery.

Rabbit droppings and rabbit scrapes are all over the place. Short grass is the most nutritious. The growth points in grasses are at the bases of the leaves, unlike in most other plants. So this is where grazers find the highest proportion of protein relative to fibre. Sheep and antelopes also exploit the nutritional advantages of short grass, while most bigger grazers are bulk feeders with big fermentation chambers for stomachs.

There are several burrows near the headstones, and outside one I find a rabbit shoulder blade (I've eaten enough rabbit stews to know what they look like) and, much more macabre, a human molar tooth and a finger bone. It seems that, round here at least, the dead don't always Rest In Peace

home to Kings and Queens
the empty palace roofless
rabbits rule here now

Letting go

When did it happen? Between one second and the next, between two very ordinary seconds.

Let's talk about it, Mother.

In the morning you were agitated, thought I'd left you, but I had just gone to fetch stuff from the car. Eyes closed, you'd tried to get out of the bed, thrown back the blanket. I came back in, soothed you, pulled up the covers. You often told me you'd once taken me to the movies, end of the war—you loved the movies. There was a baby in the film who'd thrown back his blanket. My little voice, in the smoke-filled cinema, had called out, "Keep your covers on, baby, keep your covers on." I was three then. Now I'm seventy, and it's me keeping you covered.

When the nurses came in they washed you, changed the undersheet—you'd had a little accident from the laxative, but there was nothing more going in—it would be easier now. They fitted new batteries to the driver, increased the diamorphine slightly. Although you were heavily sedated, the chief nurse said you could hear us—me, the nurses, the carers. After they left I sat with you, talking nonsense, just to prove I was still there. I kept reassuring you my brother Stephen, your third son, would arrive soon from Switzerland, although I didn't expect him until the following day. I chattered on about the weather.

> the sky today?
> there is blue, sure,
> broken clouds
>
> over the hills,
> a wall of pinkish grey
> a leaden horizon

Stephen will arrive soon, I told you, Stephen will arrive soon.

I ran a finger above your sleeping skin. Your lips were taut and dry, so I moistened a sponge stick and wiped them. Your mouth opened and you sucked on the sponge and bit the stick. I had difficulty getting it out of your mouth. I was laughing, and joking with you, but you must have been desperate for water.

And then, later in the afternoon, Stephen arrived, had caught a flight a day early, understood the urgency of my phone call. We took it in turns to sit and talk to you, with no replies of any kind. The afternoon carer came in, checked you, brushed your white hair. I made a meal, watched you until the evening carer came in, nothing much to be done. I figured you would sleep now, so we watched TV for half an hour, and then I came in to check you. Your face had changed colour, lost colour, and you looked peaceful and still. I felt your skin, and it had started to cool. At some point in the lost seconds, you had known you didn't have to wait any longer; you could let go.

Finally

For Elisabeth, Pippa, Susanne and Thaïs

I'm coming to the end of the Fellowship, the end of my four week stay in Hawthornden Castle, in the good company of four other authors, being extremely well looked after, and writing every day from breakfast to supper-time, and often before breakfast and after supper too.

I wanted to write a book, and I have. I have never been so focussed on my writing, never before had the freedom to think about nothing else but writing, and I doubt if I'll ever be the same again.

I thought I knew a bit about haibun before I came, having had several published over the years, but the experience of writing more than a hundred in four weeks has given me a far greater understanding of what a good haibun can be, and a deeper feeling for the art. I'm re-evaluating my influences, which is a good thing for a writer to do. It has also sharpened my skills in haiku and tanka writing. No more short cuts, boys and girls, no more sloppy, underwritten haiku!

The trees I look out on every day have changed considerably since I arrived. Rowan and ash have lost all their leaves, sycamore and cherry are not far behind, the birch trees have dumped thousands of leaves on the ground and in the river, but there are still a few larch left, glowing golden yellow against the dark conifers. Oak trees are thinning, and their prodigious crop of acorns, the ones left by jays and squirrels, fall from their cups with every gust of wind that shakes the boughs. Beech, now a marvellous russet colour, will retain a third of their leaves throughout the winter, but the rest will tumble by the end of the month.

What will remain? Yew, spruce, pine, a new book, and friendships with my companions here. Yesterday I paid my respects at the tomb of William Drummond of Hawthornden, former owner of this castle, and whose library formed one of the foundations of Edinburgh University Library. Tomorrow I will say goodbye and thank you to the staff here, and to my friends. By the weekend I will be home, writing with a view of the East Coast Main Line and the bungalow across the road, but seeing the steep gorge of the North Esk River, and the wonderful trees below my window.

writing every day
the view from castle window
sky, look at the sky

∾

COLIN WILL

HAWTHORNDEN CASTLE

07/11/13